TIME ZONES

1

Tim Collins
Mary Jane Maples
Ian Purdon

SECOND EDITION

 |

Australia • Brazil • Japan • Korea • Mexico • Singapore • Spain • United Kingdom • United States

Time Zones Student Book 1
Second Edition

**Tim Collins, Mary Jane Maples,
and Ian Purdon**

Publisher: Andrew Robinson

Executive Editor: Sean Bermingham

Senior Development Editor: Derek Mackrell

Development Editors: Sian Mavor,
 Charlotte Sharman

Associate Development Editor:
 Ridhima Thakral

Director of Global Marketing: Ian Martin

Product Marketing Manager: Anders Bylund

Media Researcher: Leila Hishmeh

Senior Director of Production:
 Michael Burggren

Senior Content Project Manager:
 Tan Jin Hock

Manufacturing Planner:
 Mary Beth Hennebury

Compositor: Cenveo Publisher Services

Cover/Text Design: Creative Director:
 Christopher Roy, Art Director: Scott Baker,
 Senior Designer: Michael Rosenquest

Cover Photo: Sunset at Myeong Dong, Seoul,
 South Korea: Jared Lim/500px Prime

Student Book with Online Workbook:
ISBN-13: 978-1-305-50924-5

Student Book:
ISBN-13: 978-1-305-25984-3

National Geographic Learning
20 Channel Center Street
Boston, MA 02210
USA

Cengage Learning is a leading provider of customized learning solutions with employees residing in nearly 40 different countries and sales in more than 125 countries around the world. Find your local representative at:
www.cengage.com

Cengage Learning products are represented in Canada by Nelson Education, Ltd.

Visit National Geographic Learning online at **NGL.Cengage.com**

Visit our corporate website at **www.cengage.com**

Printed in the United States of America
Print Number: 06   Print Year: 2017

Contents

SCOPE AND SEQUENCE

Unit	Functions	Grammar	Vocabulary	Pronunciation	Read, Write, & Watch
Page 6 **1** **What's Your Favorite Band?**	Talking about popular movies, books, music, bands, etc. **Real English:** *Really?*	***Wh-* questions:** *what* and *who* *What's his favorite movie?* *Who's her favorite singer?* *What's your favorite … ?*	Favorites People Sports	Contractions *What's/Who's*	**Reading:** My Favorite Things **Writing:** Short paragraph **Video:** My Favorites
Page 16 **2** **Monkeys Are Amazing!**	Identifying animal sounds Talking about favorite animals **Real English:** *Wow!*	**Adjectives:** *Are monkeys quiet?* *Jaguars are big.* *Frogs are noisy.* *Parrots are beautiful.*	Animals Adjectives	Long and short *a* sounds	**Reading:** The Amazing Aye-aye **Writing:** Poster and short description **Video:** Canopy Creatures
Page 26 **3** **Where's the Shark?**	Talking about location of things Describing ocean animals **Real English:** *Look!*	**Asking for quantity and location:** *How many fish are there?* *Where's the crab?* *Is the crab on the rock?* **Prepositions of place:** *in, on, under, between, in front of, behind, next to*	Ocean Animals Prepositions	*There are* and *They're*	**Reading:** Strange Sea Animals **Writing:** Short paragraph **Video:** Ocean Oddities
Page 36 **4** **This Is My Family.**	Introducing and identifying family members Talking about family members **Real English:** *Yeah!*	**Family members and relationships:** Verb *to have* *She has a brother.* *I have two sisters.* *Do they have any cousins?* *Do you have any brothers and sisters?*	Family	Reduction of *do* and *does*	**Reading:** Twins Days Festival **Writing:** Email **Video:** Megafamily
Page 46 **5** **I Like Fruit!**	Expressing likes and dislikes Talking about one's favorite food **Real English:** *Me too. / Me neither.*	**Expressing likes and dislikes:** *I like chips. I don't like onions.* *They like rice, but they don't like sandwiches.* *She doesn't like vegetables.* *Do you like juice?*	Food and drinks	Final *s* sounds	**Reading:** Foodscapes **Writing:** Short paragraph **Video:** A Strange Meal
Page 56 **6** **What Time Do You Go to School?**	Talking about routines and school subjects **Real English:** *See you later!*	**Simple present:** *School (always) starts at 8.* **Adverbs of frequency:** *always, usually, often, sometimes, never* **Asking about time:** *What time does school start?* *What time do you get up?*	Verbs Times School subjects	Long and short *u* sounds	**Reading:** Kakenya's Dream **Writing:** Email **Video:** Kakenya's School

WHAT'S YOUR FAVORITE BAND?

**A band playing
in concert**

Preview

A 🎧1-01 **Match.** Write the words in the box under the pictures. Listen and check your answers.

> movie   singer   band   book   ~~TV show~~

1. TV show   2. _____   3. _____   4. _____   5. _____

B 🎧1-02 **Listen to the questions.** Circle the words you hear in each question. Then listen to the whole conversation and circle the students' answers.

QUESTIONS	ANSWERS		
1. What's your favorite (**movie** /(**book**))?	*Divergent*	*Wolf Brother*	(*The Hunger Games*)
2. Who's your favorite (**singer** / **band**)?	*Taylor Swift*	*Bruno Mars*	*Pharrell Williams*
3. What's your favorite (**band** / **book**)?	*Maroon 5*	*One Direction*	*Imagine Dragons*
4. What's your favorite (**TV show** / **movie**)?	*The X Factor*	*Glee*	*The Voice*
5. What's your favorite (**movie** / **book**)?	*Godzilla*	*The Maze Runner*	*The Amazing Spider-Man*

C **Talk with a partner.** Ask and answer the questions in **B**. Take turns.

> What's your favorite movie?

> My favorite movie is *The Maze Runner*.

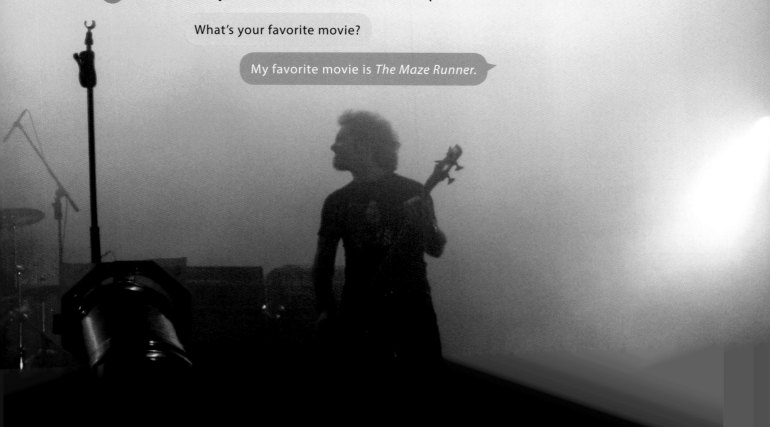

Language Focus

A 🎧 1–03 **Listen and read.** Then repeat the conversation and replace the words in **blue**.

REAL ENGLISH Really?

B **Practice with a partner.** Replace any words to make your own conversation.

1
What's your favorite book, Maya?
Wolf Brother.
That's my favorite book, too!
Divergent
The Hunger Games

2
What's your favorite TV show?
Um . . . *The X Factor*.
Really? That's my favorite TV show, too!
The Vampire Diaries
Glee

3
What's your favorite movie?
X-Men.
Hey! That's my favorite movie, too!
The Amazing Spider-Man
Twilight

4
And who's your favorite movie star?
Chris Hemsworth.
Wow! **He's** my favorite movie star, too!
Scarlett Johansson / She's
Leonardo DiCaprio / He's

🎧 1–04

TALKING ABOUT FAVORITES		
What's your favorite movie?	**My** favorite movie **is** *Godzilla*.	
What's Maya's favorite TV show?	**Her** favorite TV show **is** *The X Factor*.	What's = What is
What's his favorite band?	**His** favorite band **is** Maroon 5.	Who's = Who is
Who's her favorite singer?	**Her** favorite singer **is** Bruno Mars.	

C Write the words in the correct columns.

People	Things
movie star	song

band   color
movie   book
singer   ~~movie star~~
~~song~~   writer
TV show

D 🎧1–05 **Complete the conversations.** Write the correct words. Listen and check your answers.

1. Nadine: (1) _What's_ Ana's favorite book?

   Stig: (2) _____ favorite book is *The Hunger Games*.

   Nadine: (3) _____ her favorite writer?

   Stig: Suzanne Collins.

2. Ming: (1) _____ Carl's favorite movie star?

   Maya: (2) _____ favorite movie star is Jennifer Lawrence.

   Ming: Hey! (3) _____ my favorite movie star, too.

   (4) _____ Carl's favorite movie?

   Maya: *Guardians of the Galaxy*.

3. Stig: (1) _____ your favorite singer?

   Ming: (2) _____ favorite singer is Bruno Mars.

   Stig: What's (3) _____ favorite band?

   Ming: The Black Eyed Peas.

   Stig: Wow! That's (4) _____ favorite band, too!

E **Interview a famous person.** Work in pairs. **Student A:** Imagine you are a movie star or singer. **Student B:** Ask your partner about his or her favorite things.

Hi, Bruno Mars. What's your favorite book?

Divergent.

What's your favorite movie?

Interstellar.

The World's
Favorite
Sports

Soccer is a very popular sport. More than 3.5 billion people all over the world watch soccer. Some other popular sports are cricket, rugby, and tennis.

rugby   soccer   baseball   basketball   cricket   tennis

A 🎧1–06 **Listen to the descriptions.** Complete the sentences. Use the countries in the box.

> New Zealand   Spain   Jamaica

1. This is _____'s flag.

   This country's favorite sport is (**tennis** / **baseball**). Rafael Nadal is a very famous player.

2. This is _____'s flag.

   This country's favorite sport is (**cricket** / **basketball**). Courtney Walsh is a very famous player.

3. This is _____'s flag.

   This country's favorite sport is (**tennis** / **rugby**). The national team is the All Blacks.

B 🎧1–07 **Circle the correct answers in A.** Then listen and check your answers.

Discussion. What's your country's favorite sport? Who's a famous player?

Pronunciation

Contractions: *What's / Who's*

A 🎧1–08 **Listen and repeat.**

1. What is, What's   2. Who is, Who's

B 🎧1–09 **Listen.** Write *Who's* or *What's*.

1. _____ your favorite movie star?

2. _____ your favorite book?

3. _____ your favorite writer?

4. _____ your favorite song?

5. _____ your favorite singer?

C **Work with a partner.** Take turns to read the questions in **B**.

DO YOU KNOW?

What sport is also the name of an insect?

a. cricket
b. rugby
c. soccer

Communication

Bruno Mars

Do a class survey. Write your own questions for 4 and 5. Interview your classmates and complete the survey. Talk about the answers.

	1. What's your favorite number?	2. What's your favorite color?	3. What's your favorite song?	4. Who's _____ _____	5. What's _____ _____
Name _____	five	red	"Just the Way You Are"		
Name _____					
Name _____					

Reading

A **Read the article quickly.** What does Wesley talk about? Check (✓) all correct answers.

◯ movies　　◯ books　　◯ sports

B **Read the information about Wesley.** Underline the sports.

C **Make a list.** Write any other sports you know.

golf _____

_____

_____

MY FAVORITE
THINGS

🎧 1–10

Hi! My name is Wesley Thomas. I'm 15 years old. I'm from Kampala, Uganda. My hobbies are movies, sports, and music.

My favorite sport is soccer. I also play tennis and rugby. My favorite sports star is a tennis player. His name is Andy Murray.

5 My favorite singer is Taylor Swift. She's from the United States. My favorite movie is *Thor,* and my favorite actor is Chris Hemsworth.

Comprehension

A Answer the questions about *My Favorite Things*.

> **IDIOM**
>
> **"I'm really into . . ."**
> **means _____**
>
> a. it's my favorite . . .
> b. I really like . . .

1. Main Idea What's this article about?

   a. Kampala, Uganda   b. a movie star   c. Wesley's favorite things

2. Detail What's Wesley's favorite sport?

   a. soccer   b. tennis   c. rugby

3. Detail Andy Murray is a _____ player.

   a. cricket   b. soccer   c. tennis

4. Detail Who's Wesley's favorite singer?

   a. Beyoncé   b. Taylor Swift   c. Bruno Mars

5. Detail What's Wesley's favorite movie?

   a. *Avatar*   b. *Godzilla*   c. *Thor*

B **Complete the chart.** Write Wesley's and your favorite things.

Wesley's Favorite Things	My Favorite Things

C **CRITICAL THINKING** **Talk with a partner.** How are you and Wesley the same? How are you different?

Writing

Write a short paragraph.
Describe yourself.

My name is Carla Lopez and I'm from
Rio de Janeiro, Brazil. My favorite band is
One Direction, and Harry Styles is my
favorite singer. My favorite book is *Awaken*.
Meg Cabot is my favorite writer. My
favorite sport is tennis. My favorite player
is Rafael Nadal.

My Favorites

ABOUT THE VIDEO

Three people talk about their favorite sports.

BEFORE YOU WATCH

Circle the correct answer. What do you know about sports?

Kayaking, rock climbing, and mountain biking are all _____.

    a. team sports

    b. extreme sports

    c. water sports

WHILE YOU WATCH

A **Check your answer to the Before You Watch question.**

B **Watch the video again.** Match each person to their favorite sport.

    1. Dane   ○   ○   a. mountain biking

    2. Rebecca   ○   ○   b. rock climbing

    3. Alex   ○   ○   c. kayaking

AFTER YOU WATCH

Talk with a partner. What places do you remember from the video? What other extreme sports do you know?

A kayaker goes down a short waterfall.

MONKEYS ARE
AMAZING!

**Mona monkeys, Monkey
Sanctuary, Ghana**

Preview

A 🎧 1–11 **Listen.** Number the animals.

B 🎧 1–12 **Match.** Write the words in the box under the animals. Listen and check.

> snake   jaguar   ~~frog~~   parrot   monkey

1. _frog_   2. _____   3. _____   4. _____   5. _____

C **Talk with a partner.** What's your favorite animal on this page?

> What's your favorite animal?

> My favorite animal is the parrot.

Language Focus

A 🎧 1-13 **Listen and read.** Then repeat the conversation and replace the words in blue.

B **Practice with a partner.** Replace any words to make your own conversation.

1
This is my **parrot**. His name's Otto.

Wow! He's amazing! He's really beautiful!

lizard
frog

2
He's very **colorful**.

Yes, he is.

beautiful
small

3
Is he **noisy**?

Yes, he is. He's very **noisy**!

quiet
friendly

4
And he's really **big**! Argh!

scary
noisy

🎧 1-14

DESCRIBING ANIMALS		
Lizards **are** amazing. They**'re** quiet. They**'re not** noisy.		They're = They are They're not = They are not
Is she shy?	**Yes**, she **is**. **No**, she**'s not**.	
Are lizards beautiful?	**Yes**, they **are**. **No**, they**'re not**.	

C 🎧 1–15 **Listen.** Circle the words you hear.

1. Frogs are (**noisy** / **quiet**).
2. Jaguars are (**big** / **small**).
3. Parrots are (**ugly** / **beautiful**).
4. Monkeys are (**shy** / **friendly**).
5. Lizards are (**scary** / **beautiful**).

IDIOM

What is a "teacher's pet"?
a. the teacher's computer
b. the teacher's favorite student

D **Write questions about the animals in C.** Then ask a partner to answer them.

1. monkeys / quiet _Are monkeys quiet?_
2. frogs / shy _____
3. jaguars / friendly _____
4. parrots / quiet _____
5. lizards / beautiful _____

> Are monkeys quiet?

> Yes, they are.

E **Play a memory game.** Work in a group. Use the photos in this unit to help you.

> Jaguars are big.

> Jaguars are big, and lizards are ugly.

> Jaguars are big. Lizards are ugly, and monkeys are noisy.

Marine iguana

Animals from South America

Many amazing animals live in the rain forests of South America. Look at the pictures. Do you know any of these South American animals?

A 🎧 1–16 **Listen.** Write the names of the animals in the chart in the order you hear them. Use the words in the box.

> green iguana   howler monkey   macaw

B 🎧 1–17 **Listen.** Complete the chart. Then listen again and check your answers.

	1. _____	2. _____	3. _____
Type of . . .	_____	monkey	_____
What are they like?	beautiful and _____	black, brown, or _____	long, _____, and strong
How long do they live?	up to ____ years	up to 20 years	up to ____ years

Discussion. Describe your favorite animal.

Pronunciation
Long and short *a* sounds

A 🎧 1–18 **Listen and repeat.**

1. a, <u>a</u>nimal   2. a, n<u>a</u>me

B 🎧 1–19 **Complete the chart below.** Use the words in the box. Listen and check your answers.

> parrot   j<u>a</u>guar   s<u>a</u>me
> ~~black~~   f<u>a</u>vorite   am<u>a</u>zing

Sounds like *a* in <u>a</u>nimal	Sounds like *a* in n<u>a</u>me
black	

C **Work with a partner.** Take turns to read the words in **B**.

DO YOU KNOW?

This lizard is really small. It is the size of a coin. Where's it from?

a. Madagascar
b. Thailand
c. Brazil

Communication

Play a true-false game. Work with a partner. Take turns to describe an animal.
Student A: Say two true sentences and one false sentence.
Student B: Guess the false sentence.

Tigers are orange and black.

That's true!

Tigers are from Africa.

That's false! They're from Asia!

Tiger

An aye-aye in his nest, Madagascar

Reading

A **Look at the photo.** Check (✓) all the facts you think are true.

◯ This animal is big.   ◯ This animal is fast.   ◯ This animal is shy.

B **Read the article quickly.** Underline the adjectives.

C **Read again.** Where do aye-ayes live?

THE AMAZING AYE-AYE

🎧 1–20

This <u>amazing</u> animal is an aye-aye. It's from Madagascar. It lives in the rain forest.

Aye-ayes are black or brown. They are very small. Their tails are long. Their eyes are big and so are their ears. They have really long, strong
5 fingers. They catch food with their fingers. When they move, they're not fast—they're very slow.

Some people think aye-ayes are scary because they look strange. But aye-ayes are friendly animals!

Comprehension

A **Answer the questions about *The Amazing Aye-Aye.***

1. `Main Idea` What is this article about?

    a. Madagascar

    b. rain forests

    c. a strange animal

2. `Detail` What color are aye-ayes?

    a. brown or black

    b. black or white

    c. brown or grey

3. `Detail` Aye-ayes catch food with their long _____.

    a. hands

    b. tails

    c. fingers

4. `Detail` People think aye-ayes are scary because _____.

    a. they are slow

    b. they are small

    c. they look strange

5. `Detail` Aye-ayes are NOT _____.

    a. small

    b. fast

    c. friendly

B **Label the picture.** Use the words in the box.

> ear   eye   tail   finger

C **CRITICAL THINKING** **Talk with a partner.** Do you think aye-ayes are scary?

Writing

Make a poster about an amazing animal. Find a photo of the animal. Then show your poster to the class.

Jaguar

This big cat is called a jaguar. It lives in the rain forests. It is orange and white. It has black spots. It's very strong and fast. It's also shy. Some people think jaguars are scary.

Canopy Creatures

ABOUT THE VIDEO

Many interesting animals live in the forest on Barro Colorado Island, Panama.

BEFORE YOU WATCH

Look at the photo. Which animals do you think are in this rain forest? Make a list.

_____

WHILE YOU WATCH

A **Check.** What animals on your list did you see?

B **Watch the video again.** Complete the sentences using the words in the box.

> noisy   big   small   long

1. The rain forest on the island of Barro Colorado is very _____.

2. The howler monkey is really _____.

3. The coati's tail is very _____.

4. The red-eyed tree frog is _____.

AFTER YOU WATCH

Talk with a partner. What animals live in rain forests? What interesting animals do you know?

A capuchin monkey in a rain forest

WHERE'S THE
SHARK?

A reef shark and
reef fish at Beqa
Island, Fiji

Preview

A 🎧 1–21 **Listen.** Circle the words you hear.

1. The dolphin is (**quiet** / **beautiful**).

2. The fish is (**big** / **colorful**).

3. The ray is (**quiet** / **colorful**).

4. The shark is (**small** / **scary**).

B **Complete the sentences.** Look at the photos. Use the words from the box.

quiet	big	small	beautiful	slow
shy	friendly	colorful	fast	scary

1. Dolphins are _friendly and beautiful_.

2. Rays are _____.

3. Fish are _____.

4. Sharks are _____.

C **Talk with a partner.** Read your sentences in **B**.

Dolphins are shy and quiet.

No, they're not! They're friendly and noisy.

ray

dolphin

Language Focus

A 🎧 1–22 **Listen and read.** Then repeat the conversation and replace the words in **blue**.

B **Practice with a partner.** Replace any words to make your own conversation.

🎧 1–23

TALKING ABOUT LOCATION OF THINGS

The fish is near the crab.
The shark is behind the seaweed.

How many sea animals **are there**?	**There's** one (sea animal). **There are** 20 (sea animals).
Where's the crab?	It's **on** / **under** / **next to** the rock.
Where are the sharks?	They're **in front of** / **behind** the rock.
Is the crab **on** the rock?	Yes, it is. / No, it's not.
Are the fish **in** the seaweed?	Yes, they are. / No, they're not.

C **Look at picture 1 in the cartoon on page 28.** Answer the questions.

1. How many dolphins are there? <u>There's one dolphin.</u>

2. How many colorful fish are there? _____

3. How many sharks are there? _____

4. How many crabs are there? _____

D **Look at the picture at the bottom of this page.** Complete the sentences. Use words from the box.

in	on	behind
between	under	in front of

1. The seahorse is _____ the rock.

2. The crab is _____ the seaweed.

3. The octopus is _____ the shark.

4. The starfish is _____ the sand.

5. The fish are _____ the water.

6. The sea turtle is _____ the starfish and the crab.

E **Play a game.** Work in pairs. **Student A:** Choose something in the classroom. **Student B:** Guess what it is.

Is it on the table?

Yes, it is.

DO YOU KNOW?

What is this?
a. a catfish
b. a horsefish
c. a dogfish

SAVE THE OCEAN

Mariana Fuentes is a National Geographic Young Explorer. She studies sea animals, like sea turtles and dugongs. One of her favorite places is the Torres Strait near Australia. She looks after turtles on the beach.

A **Read the information about Mariana Fuentes.** Then answer the questions.

1. Mariana studies (**sea turtles** / **dolphins**).

2. One of her favorite places is (**the Torres Strait** / **France**).

3. She looks after turtles (**on the beach** / **in the sea**).

B 🎧 1–24 **Listen.** Circle **T** for True or **F** for False.

1. There are seven kinds of sea turtles. T F

2. Leatherback sea turtles are really small. T F

3. Dugongs live up to 100 years. T F

4. Dugongs are also called sea cows. T F

Discussion. What sea animal do you want to look after? Why?

A sea turtle

A dugong

Pronunciation

There are and *They're*

A 🎧 1-25 **Listen and repeat.**

1. There are   2. They're

B 🎧 1-26 **Listen.** Circle *There are* or *They're*.

1. (**There are** / **They're**) 800 fish in the tank.

2. (**There are** / **They're**) in the seaweed.

3. (**There are** / **They're**) between two rocks.

4. (**There are** / **They're**) seven kinds of sea turtles.

5. (**There are** / **They're**) two crabs on the rock.

C **Work with a partner.** Take turns to read the sentences in **B**.

Communication

| jaguar | sea turtle | dolphin | shark | crab | howler monkey |

Draw and ask. Choose four animals from the box above and draw them on the beach picture. Ask a partner questions about the animals in his or her picture. Then draw your partner's picture on page 130. Compare the pictures.

What animals are in your picture? Is there a shark?

Yes, there's a shark.

Where is it?

It's behind the seaweed.

Leafy seadragon

Reading

A **Look at the pictures.** What things do you see? Check (✓) them.

⬡ seaweed   ⬡ rocks   ⬡ fish

B **Read the title.** Why do you think these animals are strange?

C **Read the article quickly.** Underline the places where the animals hide.

STRANGE SEA ANIMALS

🎧 1–27

Do you know that some animals are camouflaged? This means their color is the same as the colors around them. Some camouflaged animals hide in seaweed, rocks, and sand.

5 Look at the photo on the left. This looks like seaweed, but it's not! It's the leafy seadragon. It hides in the seaweed. Its the same color as the seaweed. Like the seaweed, its body is also in the shape of a leaf.

Look at the photo below. This is a stonefish. It hides on the sand, near rocks. It looks like a rock. Where are its eyes and its mouth?

Stonefish

Comprehension

A **Answer the questions about _Strange Sea Animals_.**

1. Main Idea   What's this article about?

   a. jungle animals   b. animals that hide   c. endangered animals

2. Vocabulary   When animals hide in the same colors around them they are _____.

   a. covered   b. camouflaged   c. trapped

3. Detail   In line 6, "its" refers to _____.

   a. a leaf   b. seaweed   c. the leafy seadragon

4. Detail   A stonefish hides _____.

   a. on the sand   b. under the sand   c. under the rocks

5. Detail   A stonefish looks like _____.

   a. seaweed   b. a rock   c. a seadragon

B **Complete the chart.**

What are their names?	What do they look like?	Where do they hide?
stonefish leafy seadragon		

C CRITICAL THINKING   **Talk with a partner.** What other animals use camouflage to hide?

Writing

Write a short paragraph. Find a photo of a sea animal. Then write about the animal.

Whale sharks live in the oceans around the world. They are brown, grey, and white. Their mouths are big. They eat small fish and plants. They are really big and look beautiful.

Ocean Oddities

ABOUT THE VIDEO

Many strange creatures live in the ocean.

BEFORE YOU WATCH

What sea animals do you know? Make a list.

_____

WHILE YOU WATCH

A **Check.** What animals on your list did you see?

B **Watch the video again.** Circle the words you hear.

1. Sargassum fish hide in (**seaweed** / **coral**).

2. Comb jellyfish are (**colorful** / **bright**).

3. Beluga whales are very (**quiet** / **noisy**).

4. Clams use their (**foot** / **tongue**) to push into the sand.

AFTER YOU WATCH

Talk with a partner. Describe the sea animals in the video. Are there strange animals in your country? Describe them.

Fish swimming near coral, Red Sea, Egypt

4

THIS IS MY FAMILY.

Preview

A 🎧1-28 **Look at the photo.** How many people are in this family? Listen and check your answer.

B **Match the words with the numbers.** Use the words in the box.

> mom   dad   brother   sister

1. _____   2. _____   3. _____   4. _____

C **Talk to a partner.** Ask and answer questions.

> How many people are there in your family?

> There are five people in my family.

The Cason family

37

Language Focus

A 🎧1–29 **Listen and read.** Then repeat the conversation, and replace the words in blue.

REAL ENGLISH Yeah!

B **Practice with a partner.** Replace any words to make your own conversation.

1 Hey, Maya—are those your family photos?

Yes, this is my family in Brazil. That's my dad and that's my mom.

Nadine / South Africa
Stig / Sweden

2 Are these your sisters?

No, they're my cousins.

friends
brothers

3 OK. Do you have any brothers and sisters?

Yeah! I have a brother and two sisters.

three
four

4 Is that your baby brother?

No, that's me!

baby sister
cousin

🎧1–30

TALKING ABOUT FAMILY MEMBERS		
I **have** two sisters. She **has** a brother. They **have** a brother.		
Do you have any brothers and sisters?	Yes, I **do**. No, I **don't**.	do not = don't does not = doesn't
Does she **have** a brother?	Yes, she **does**. No, she **doesn't**.	
Do they **have** any cousins?	Yes, they **do**. No, they **don't**.	

C 🎧1–31 **Circle the correct answer.** Listen and check.

1. Do you have a brother?   Yes, I (**do** / **does**).
2. Does she have a sister?   No, she (**don't** / **doesn't**).
3. Does he have a daughter?   Yes, he (**does** / **do**).
4. Do they have any brothers or sisters?   Yes, they (**does** / **do**).
5. Do you have any children?   No, I (**doesn't** / **don't**).

D **Complete the questions.** Write *Do* or *Does*. Then look at the photo below and answer the questions.

1. _____ Sarah have a husband?   _____

2. _____ Jason and Peter have two sisters?   _____

3. _____ Lisa have two brothers?   _____

4. _____ Chris and Sarah have children?   _____

5. _____ Peter have a sister?   _____

E **Work with a partner.** Ask and answer questions to make your partner's family tree. Look at Lisa's family tree on page 130 to help you.

Family Life

Do you know the difference between your immediate family and your extended family? Your immediate family includes your father, mother, and brothers and sisters. Your extended family includes other family members such as aunts, uncles, and cousins.

A Write the words in the correct circle.

aunt	brother
children	~~cousin~~
dad	daughter
grandmother	niece
grandfather	~~mom~~
parents	sister
son	nephew
grandparents	

Extended Family

cousin

Immediate Family

mom

B 🎧1-32 **Answer the questions.** Then listen and check your answers.

1. Who's your brother's mom?   She's my _____.

2. Who's your uncle's daughter?   She's my _____.

3. Who's your dad's dad?   He's my _____.

4. Who's your sister's daughter?   She's my _____.

5. Who's your father's brother?   He's my _____.

6. Who's your mom's sister?   She's my _____.

Discussion. Do you want to live with your immediate family or with your extended family? Give reasons.

Pronunciation

Reduction: *do* and *does*

A 🎧 1-33 **Listen and repeat.**

1. Do you have a sister?
2. Do they have cousins?
3. Does he have a brother?
4. Does he have an aunt?
5. Does she have a nephew?
6. Does he have a niece?

B 🎧 1-34 **Listen and answer.** Circle the words you hear.

1. (**Does she / Do they**) have a cousin?
2. (**Do they / Do you**) have an aunt?
3. (**Do they / Does he**) have younger brothers?
4. (**Does she / Do they**) have a baby sister?
5. (**Do they / Does she**) have aunts and uncles?

C **Work with a partner.** Take turns to read the sentences in **B**.

DO YOU KNOW?

Twins **are brothers or sisters who** _____.

a. are born on the same day
b. look like each other

Communication

Play a game. Ask questions from the game board below. When someone answers "Yes", write their name in the box. The first person to complete all the boxes is the winner.

> Do you have a big family?

> No, I don't.

Find someone who . . .

. . . has a big family. _____	. . . has a pet fish. _____	. . . has a brother and sister. _____
. . . has two brothers. _____	. . . has four cousins. _____	. . . has two sisters. _____
. . . has three aunts. _____	. . . has a brother. _____	. . . has a dog and cat. _____
. . . has a small family. _____	. . . has two uncles. _____	. . . has four grandparents. _____

Reading

A **Look at the photos.** What do you think the article is about? Check (✓) the correct answer.

◯ big families ◯ brothers and sisters ◯ famous families

B **Read the article quickly.** <u>Underline</u> the name of the town.

C **Make a list.** Write the names of any interesting festivals you know.

TWINS DAYS FESTIVAL

🎧 1–35

Every year, the small town of Twinsburg, Ohio, in the United States, has a special festival. It's called the Twins Days Festival. The festival takes place in August. It's three days long, and is very popular.

5 Thousands of brothers and sisters visit this festival. Most of them are twins. They go there to meet old friends and to make new ones.

Twins often look the same, with the same color hair and eyes, but sometimes there are quite a few differences. Identical twins, however, look exactly like each other. They also often have the same hobbies!

Twins at the Twins Days Festival

Comprehension

A Answer the questions about *Twins Days Festival*.

1. `Main Idea` What's another title for this article?

   a. A Special Festival   b. Visiting Ohio   c. A Day Out with Friends

2. `Detail` The festival is _____ days long.

   a. two   b. three   c. four

3. `Vocabulary` The word "popular" means people _____ . (line 3)

   a. like it   b. don't like it   c. think it's very long

4. `Inference` Who can go to this festival?

   a. everyone   b. only twins   c. only twins from Ohio

5. `Vocabulary` What is the word for twins who look exactly the same?

   a. identical   b. similar   c. different

> **IDIOM**
>
> My sister and I have red hair. It _____ in the family.
>
> a. runs
> b. walks
> c. takes

B Complete the word web.

Every
1. _____

When?

Where?
4. _____

Twins Days Festival

Why?

Who goes?

Meet
2. _____
friends

Make
3. _____
friends

Brothers and
5. _____

C CRITICAL THINKING **Talk with a partner.** Do you know any twins? Are they the same or different?

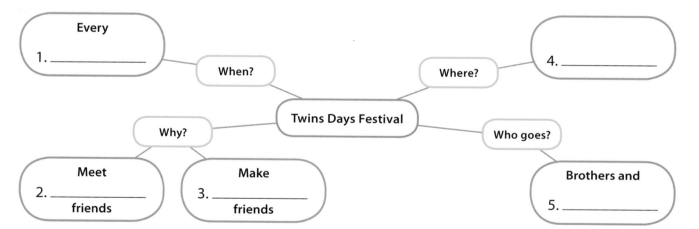

From: **Joe**   To: **Emily**

Subject: Hello from London!

Hi,

My name is Joe Parker. I'm 14 years old and I live in London, in the United Kingdom. My mom's name is Julie, and my dad's name is Steven. I have one brother. His name is Andrew. He's 12 years old.

Joe

Writing

Write an email about your family.

VIDEO

Megafamily

ABOUT THE VIDEO

The Casons talk about life in a big family.

BEFORE YOU WATCH

Circle the words you think you will hear to describe the Cason family.

happy small big fun unusual

WHILE YOU WATCH

A **Check your answers to the Before You Watch question.**

B **Watch the video again.** Circle **T** for True or **F** for False.

1. Life in a big family is difficult.	T	F
2. All children in the Cason family go to the same school.	T	F
3. All children have their own bedrooms.	T	F
4. The younger brothers and sisters fight a lot.	T	F
5. Dave Cason says his family is happy.	T	F

AFTER YOU WATCH

Talk with a partner. Do you know any big families? What are they like? Do you want to have a big family?

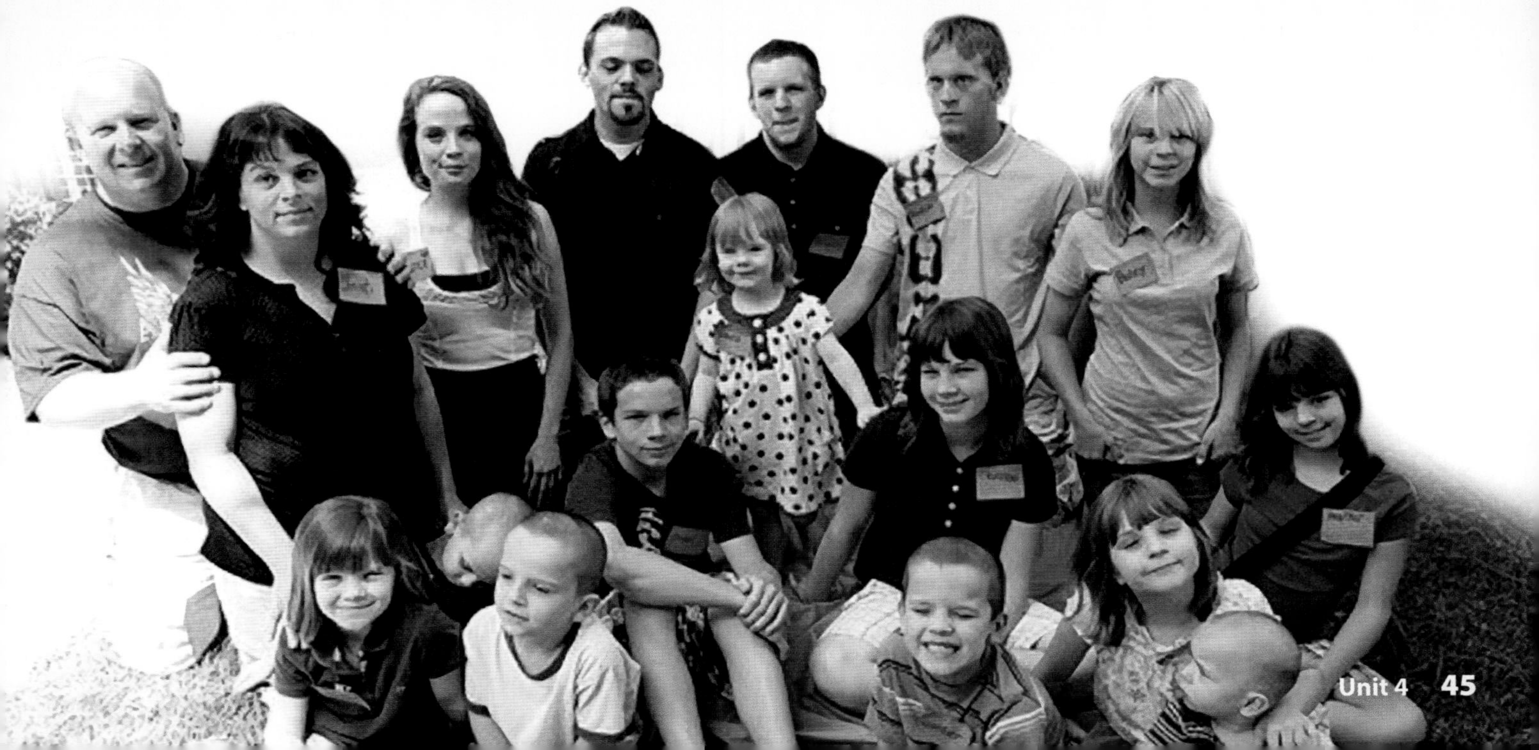

The Cason family

5

I LIKE FRUIT!

oranges

grapes

strawberries

mangoes

apples

A fruit market in South Tyrol, Italy

Preview

A 🎧 1–36 **Listen to the students.** What kind of fruit do they like? Complete the *Like* column.

NAME	LIKE ☺	DON'T LIKE ☹
Dino	apples	
Sophie		
Teresa		
Peter		oranges

B 🎧 1–37 **Listen.** What fruits don't the students like? Complete the *Don't Like* column.

C **Talk with a partner.** What foods do you like? What foods don't you like?

> I like apples, but I don't like carrots.

> I like fruit, but I don't like vegetables.

Language Focus

A 🎧 1–38 **Listen and read.** Then repeat the conversation and replace the words in **blue**.

REAL ENGLISH Me, too. / Me neither.

B **Practice with a partner.** Replace any words to make your own conversation.

🎧 1–39

TALKING ABOUT LIKES AND DISLIKES	
I **like** fruit. I **don't like** vegetables.	
They **like** rice, but they **don't like** sandwiches.	
He **likes** pizza. She **doesn't like** vegetables.	
Do you **like** juice?	Yes, I do. / No, I don't.
Does he **like** oranges?	Yes, he does. / No, he doesn't.

Countable	Uncountable
sandwich(**es**)	milk
dessert(**s**)	soup
vegetable(**s**)	bread

C **Countable or uncountable?** Are the foods below countable or uncountable? Write **C** for countable and **U** for uncountable.

popcorn ＿＿＿＿   burger ＿＿＿＿   sandwich ＿＿＿＿   soda ＿＿＿＿

bread ＿＿＿＿   chips ＿＿＿＿   rice ＿＿＿＿   soup ＿＿＿＿

pizza ＿＿＿＿   vegetables ＿＿＿＿   milk ＿＿＿＿   chocolate ＿＿＿＿

D 🎧1–40   **Complete the conversation.** Write *like* or *likes*. Then listen and check your answers.

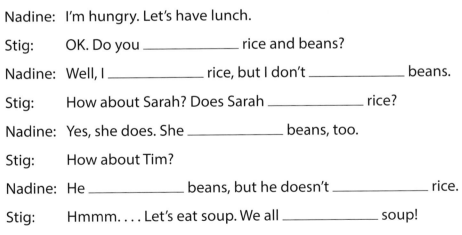

Nadine: I'm hungry. Let's have lunch.

Stig: OK. Do you ＿＿＿＿＿＿＿ rice and beans?

Nadine: Well, I ＿＿＿＿＿＿ rice, but I don't ＿＿＿＿＿＿ beans.

Stig: How about Sarah? Does Sarah ＿＿＿＿＿＿ rice?

Nadine: Yes, she does. She ＿＿＿＿＿＿ beans, too.

Stig: How about Tim?

Nadine: He ＿＿＿＿＿＿ beans, but he doesn't ＿＿＿＿＿＿ rice.

Stig: Hmmm. . . . Let's eat soup. We all ＿＿＿＿＿＿ soup!

E **Play tic-tac-toe.** Turn to page 131 and follow the instructions.

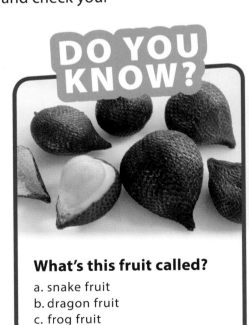

DO YOU KNOW?

What's this fruit called?
a. snake fruit
b. dragon fruit
c. frog fruit

Human Footprint

In a lifetime, we eat and drink a lot. But how many things does one person eat and drink? What is our *human footprint?*

Things consumed by average Americans in their lifetime

A **Write.** Complete the table with the words from the box.

> pizza   candy   milk   ~~soda~~   bread   chocolate

 a glass of	a slice of	a bar of	a can of
			soda

B 🎧 1–41 **Listen.** Circle the correct words. Then listen again and check your answers.

In an average lifetime Americans eat and drink about . . .

1. 14,500 bars of (**candy** / **chocolate**).
2. 5,000 (**bananas** / **apples**).
3. 43,000 cans of (**soda** / **milk**).
4. 87,000 slices of (**pizza** / **bread**).
5. 26,000 glasses of (**milk** / **water**).

Discussion. Talk about the things you eat and drink.

Pronunciation
Final s sounds

A 🎧1-42 **Listen and repeat.**

1. s, drink**s**   2. s, banana**s**   3. s, glass**es**

IDIOM

He's "the big cheese" means he's a _____.

a. very noisy person
b. very important person

B 🎧1-43 **Complete the chart.** Use the words in the box.
Then listen and check your answers.

> chips   peaches   grapes   desserts
> oranges   slices   vegetables likes

Sounds like *s* in *drinks*	Sounds like *s* in *bananas*	Sounds like *s* in *glass<u>es</u>*

C **Work with a partner.** Take turns to read the words in **B**.

Communication

Make a menu. Complete the table below. In groups, discuss food you like and don't like.
Then turn to page 131 and follow the instructions.

Meal	I Like	I Don't Like
Breakfast		
Lunch		
Dinner		

A coral seascape

Reading

A **Look at the photos.** What are these photos made from? Check (✓) the correct answer.

○ animals   ○ food   ○ paper

B **Read the article quickly.** Underline the food words.

C **Discuss with a partner.** Look at the photo with Warner. Think of a title for the photo.

FOODSCAPES

🎧 1–44

Carl Warner takes photos of interesting things. He also makes beautiful landscapes using food. These are called "foodscapes". It takes Warner four or five days to make each foodscape.

Look carefully at the photo with sea animals. What do you see?
5   There's an ocean with a lot of fish and rocks. There's seaweed, and there are sea animals. There's also sand. But what are the fish made from? The fish are made from fruit. There's an island and some trees. The trees are made from pineapples. In fact it's all made from food—fruit and vegetables! What other foods do you see in the photo? Do
10   you see apples and oranges? Now look at the photo with Warner. What foods do you see in that photo?

Carl Warner

Comprehension

A **Answer the questions about *Foodscapes*.**

1. `Main Idea` What is the article about?

   a. photos made using food   b. how to make photos   c. sea animals

2. `Inference` What is Carl Warner's job?

   a. photographer   b. gardener   c. cook

3. `Vocabulary` What does the word "landscape" mean? (line 2)

   a. how an area looks   b. how a city looks   c. a painting

4. `Detail` How long does it take Warner to make each foodscape?

   a. 2 or 3 days   b. 4 or 5 days   c. 1 week

5. `Detail` What are the trees made out of?

   a. apples   b. oranges   c. pineapples

B **Complete the word web.**

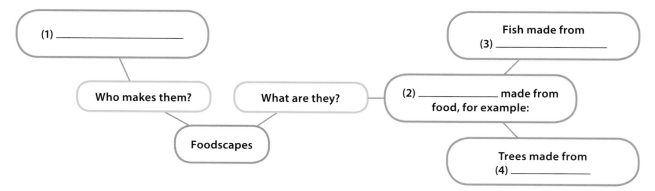

(1) _____

Who makes them?

What are they?

Foodscapes

Fish made from (3) _____

(2) _____ made from food, for example:

Trees made from (4) _____

C **CRITICAL THINKING** **Talk with a partner.** How can you make a similar picture? What fruit and vegetables do you need? Draw the picture.

Writing

Write a short paragraph. Describe your favorite traditional food.

Hi. I'm Mario. I'm from Italy. My favorite traditional food is pasta primavera. It's pasta with a lot of fresh vegetables and cheese. It's really delicious.

A Strange Meal

ABOUT THE VIDEO

A hotel in New York hosts a very interesting dinner.

BEFORE YOU WATCH

Look at the photo. Why do you think the meal in this video is strange?

WHILE YOU WATCH

A **Check your answer to the Before You Watch question.**

B **Watch the video again.** Answer these questions.

1. Gene Rurka is a _____.

   a. hotel owner   b. chef

2. What do the people at the meal eat?

   a. strange creatures   b. vegetables that look like insects

3. What does Gene say about this meal?

   a. It's dangerous.   b. It's tasty.

4. What do the people think about the food?

   a. They think it's bad.   b. They think it's good.

AFTER YOU WATCH

Talk with a partner. What food in the video is strange? Do you want to eat the food in the video?

Gene Rurka at the
Explorers Club Dinner

6

WHAT TIME DO YOU GO TO
SCHOOL?

Preview

A **Match.** Write the expressions in the box under the pictures.

> go to school   go to bed   do homework   get up   go home   have dinner

1. _____ 2. _____ 3. _____ 4. _____ 5. _____ 6. _____

B 🎧1–45 **Complete the chart.** Listen to three students talking about their school day. Write the correct times in the chart.

ACTIVITY	PAULO	IRA	THEO	YOU
get up	6:30	6 o'clock		
go to school		8 o'clock		
go home			3:30	
do homework	2 o'clock	3 o'clock	5 o'clock	
have dinner				
go to bed	9 o'clock		9:30	

C **Complete the chart for you.** Then compare your answers with a partner.

> What time do you get up?

> I get up at 6 o'clock.

College students study
outside, Seattle, U.S.A.

57

Language Focus

A 🎧 1–46 **Listen and read.** Then repeat the conversation and replace the words in blue.

REAL ENGLISH   See you later.

B **Practice with a partner.** Replace any words to make your own conversation.

🎧 1–47

TALKING ABOUT ROUTINES		
What time **do** you **get up**?	I **always** get up at 7 o'clock.	0% • never
When **do** you **have** breakfast?	I **usually** have breakfast at 7:30. I **often** have breakfast at 6:45.	• sometimes
When **does** he **do homework**?	**Sometimes** he does homework at 1:15, and **sometimes** he does it at 2:30.	• often
What time **does** school **start**?	It starts at 8 o'clock.	• usually
When **do** they **go home**?	They go home at 4 o'clock. They're **never** late.	100% • always

C **1–48** **Complete the sentences.** Then listen and check your answers.

1. She always (**get** / **gets**) up at 8 o'clock.

2. He sometimes (**has** / **have**) breakfast at 7:15.

3. What time do they (**has** / **have**) dinner?

4. What time (**do** / **does**) he go to bed?

5. I always (**do** / **does**) homework at 4 o'clock.

6. He often (**go** / **goes**) home at 6 o'clock.

IDIOM

If you do something "against the clock" you do it _____ .

a. in a hurry
b. very late

D **Complete the sentences.** Use words from the box to make true sentences about *you*.

> always   never   sometimes   often   usually

1. I _____ get up at 6 o'clock.

2. I _____ have breakfast before school.

3. I _____ do my homework after school.

4. I _____ go to bed at midnight.

E **Work in small groups.** Choose one activity and one time and make a sentence. Say how often you do the activity. Take turns.

Activity	Adverb	Time
get up	never	1:30
have breakfast	sometimes	3:00
go to school	often	6:00
go home	usually	7:30
do homework	always	8:00
go to bed		9:00

I usually get up at 6 o'clock.

What Time Is It?

Different places around the world have different times.
These are called time zones. Look at the chart. To
calculate the time you have to subtract or add the hours
to Greenwich Mean Time (GMT). Look at the chart.

A **Calculate.** It's 2 p.m. in London (GMT). What time is it in these cities?

1. Los Angeles   _6:00 a.m._   5. Nairobi   _____

2. New York   _____   6. New Delhi   _____

3. Rio de Janeiro   _____   7. Jakarta   _____

4. Madrid   _____   8. Sydney   _____

B 🎧1–49 **Quiz.** Guess the answers. Circle **T** for True or **F** for False. Then listen and check.

1. Large countries always have at least two time zones.   **T**   **F**

2. There is a country that has 12 time zones.   **T**   **F**

3. Some countries change their time when the season changes.   **T**   **F**

4. Sometimes a country changes its time zone permanently.   **T**   **F**

Discussion. Do you think time zones are a good idea? Why do you think countries
don't all use the same time zone?

Pronunciation
Long and short _u_ sounds

A 🎧1-50 **Listen and repeat.**

1. u, lunch   2. u, usually

B 🎧1-51 **Write and check.** Write the words in the chart below.
Then listen and check your answers.

> ~~computer~~   ~~hungry~~   music   student
> subject   understand   up

Sounds like _u_ in _lunch_	Sounds like _u_ in _usually_
hungry	computer

C **Work with a partner.** Take turns to read the words in **B**.

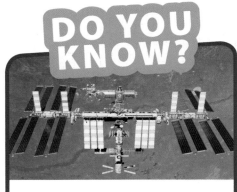
Communication

Do a survey. Write the times you do these activities. Then find two other students who do the activities at the same time as you.

What time do you . . . ?	you	student name	student name
have breakfast			
go home			
do homework			
watch TV on school days			
go to bed on school days			
go to bed on the weekends			
have dinner			

What time do you have breakfast?

I have breakfast at 7:00 o'clock.

Me, too!

Reading

A **Look at the photo.** What do you think the article is about?

    a. city life   b. a big family   c. a school in Kenya

B **Read the article quickly.** What is Kakenya's dream?

    a. to write books

    b. to help educate Maasai girls

    c. to help girls get married

C **Discuss with a partner.** Look at the subjects below. Which subjects do you think the girls study?

 math   English   science   PE   art   music   geography

KAKENYA'S DREAM

🎧 1–52

In Kenya, school life is not easy for some local Maasai people. In some schools, classes have 70 students in one classroom. Schools don't always have books. There sometimes aren't enough teachers, or there isn't enough money.

5 This is especially true for Maasai girls. Not many Maasai girls in Kenya finish elementary school. Many Maasai girls leave school early to get married. Kakenya Ntaiya has a dream. She wants to help Maasai schoolgirls. She has an elementary school for girls.

Today, 170 girls go to her school, and they love it. They study English
10 and Swahili (an African language). They also study math, science, geography, history, art, and PE. Ntaiya wants the students to have a better life.

Kakenya and her students
outside Kakenya's school

Comprehension

A Answer the questions about *Kakenya's Dream*.

1. Main Idea What is another title for this article?

   a. Life after School   b. Living in Kenya   c. A School for Girls

2. Detail How many students are there in some village school classrooms?

   a. 70   b. 90   c. 100

3. Inference Many schools in Kenya need more _____.

   a. chairs   b. teachers   c. students

4. Vocabulary "Especially true" means _____. (line 5)

   a. not true   b. only true   c. more often true

5. Detail Why do some Maasai girls not finish school?

   a. They move house.   b. They get married.   c. They leave Kenya.

B **Complete the diagram.** Look at the school subjects on page 62. Compare the school subjects at Kakenya's school with your school subjects.

Your school subjects	Both	Subjects at Kakenya's school
		Swahili

C **CRITICAL THINKING** **Talk with a partner.** What do you think of Kakenya's school? Is your school similar to or different from Kakenya's?

Writing

Write a short email. Describe your school to an online friend.

From: Eva   To: anna.smith@mail.com

Subject: School life

Hi Anna,

Let me tell you about my school life. I usually get up at 6:30, and I go to school at 7:30.

There are 600 students at my school in Quito. I study seven subjects: Spanish, English, science, history, geography, math, and computer science. School always finishes at 12:30, and then I eat lunch at home.

Eva

Kakenya's School

BEFORE YOU WATCH

Circle the correct answers. What do you already know about Kakenya's school?

1. This school is in (**Kenya** / **Uganda**).

2. The school is for girls living in (**cities** / **villages**).

WHILE YOU WATCH

A Check your answers to the Before You Watch questions.

B Watch the video again. Circle **T** for True or **F** for False.

	T	F
1. Kakenya's students live in the school.	T	F
2. They cook their own food in school.	T	F
3. School starts at 9 o'clock.	T	F
4. They study math and geography.	T	F

AFTER YOU WATCH

Talk with a partner. How would you describe Kakenya? Do you think these girls will have a better life?

Kakenya with students

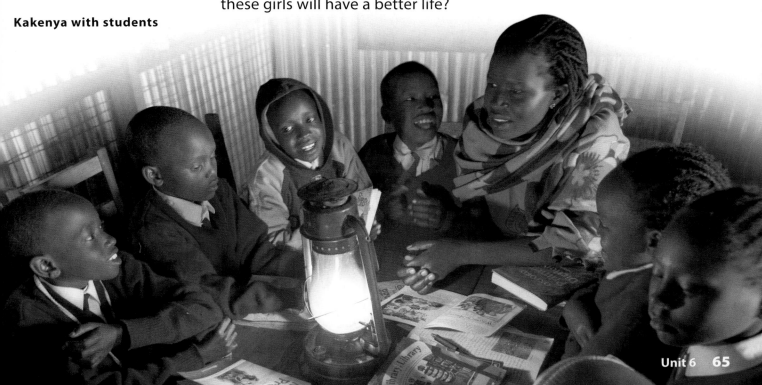

Review Game 1

Play with 2–4 classmates. Take turns. Each classmate has a game counter. Toss a coin and move your counter.

Heads = move two squares
Tails = move one square

Can't answer? Miss a turn!

START!

1. What's Maya's favorite movie?

2. Who's your favorite band or singer?

3. Which country's favorite sport is rugby?

4. What sport is also the name of an insect?

5. Otto is Stig's _____.

6. Unscramble these words: w o e r h l y m n e o k (Clue: It's a noisy animal.)

7. How long do macaws live?

8. Describe aye-ayes.

9. Say where three things are in your classroom.

10. Name three sea animals.

11. Name an animal that hides in things of the same color.

12. What is this sea animal?

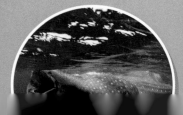

13. How many people are in the Cason family?

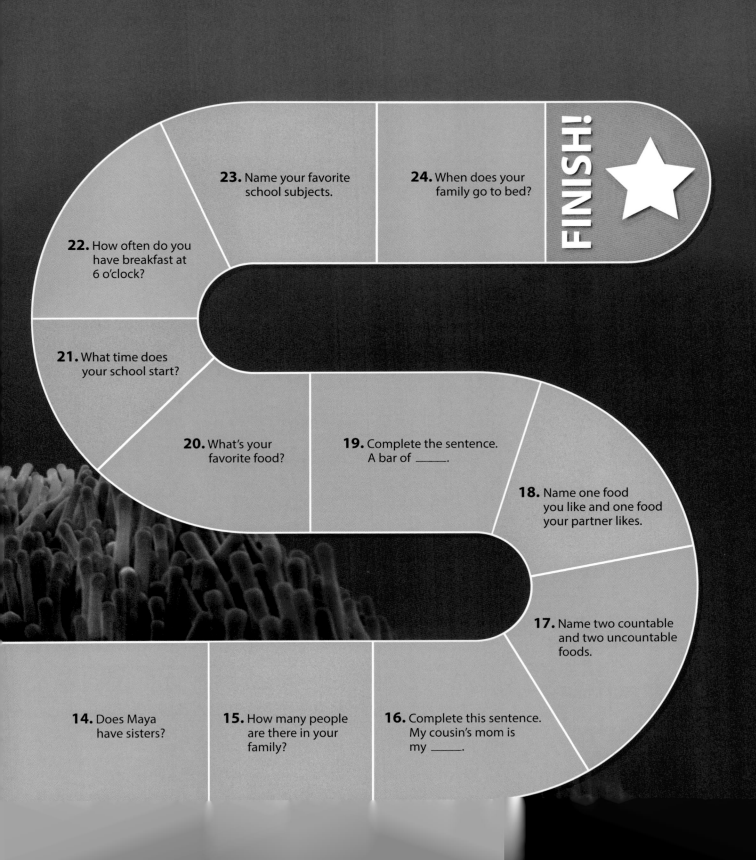

23. Name your favorite school subjects.

24. When does your family go to bed?

FINISH!

22. How often do you have breakfast at 6 o'clock?

21. What time does your school start?

20. What's your favorite food?

19. Complete the sentence. A bar of _____.

18. Name one food you like and one food your partner likes.

17. Name two countable and two uncountable foods.

14. Does Maya have sisters?

15. How many people are there in your family?

16. Complete this sentence. My cousin's mom is my _____.

CAN SQUIRRELS SKI?

Preview

A 🎧 2–01 **Guess.** What do you think these animals can do? Write the animals under the correct pictures. Then listen and check your answers.

| monkeys | parrots | squirrels | elephants | jaguars |

 water-ski

 sing

 paint

 play the piano

 swim

_____ _____ _____ _____ _____

B **CRITICAL THINKING** **Sort the actions.** Put them into the two groups below.

SPORTS	ARTS
water-ski	paint

C **Talk with a partner.** What can you do?

Can you play the piano?

No, I can't.

An elephant painting a picture

Twiggy, the water-skiing squirrel

Language Focus

REAL ENGLISH Sure!

B **Practice with a partner.** Replace any words to make your own conversation.

🎧 2–03

TALKING ABOUT ABILITIES		
I **can** ski and surf.		
Can you swim?	Yes, I **can**. / No, I **can't**.	
What **can** parrots do?	They **can** sing, but they **can't** play the piano.	can't = cannot
Can he play baseball?	No, he **can't**, but he **can** play golf.	

70 Unit 7

C 🎧 2–04 **Complete the conversation.** Write *can* or *can't*. Listen and check your answers.

Nadine: Hey Stig, look at this! It's a painting by Phong the elephant. Phong is from Thailand.

Stig: Wow! (1) _____ elephants paint?

Nadine: Not usually, but Phong (2) _____ . Phong (3) _____ play music, too.

Stig: Amazing! What other things (4) _____ Phong do? (5) _____ he dance?

Nadine: No, he (6) _____ dance, and he (7) _____ skateboard either. He's an elephant!

D **Check (✓) the things you can do.** Then ask a partner.

CAN YOU_____?	YOU	YOUR PARTNER
🕺 dance		
🤸 do a handstand		
🛹 skateboard		
🥁 play the drums		
🚗 drive		

E **Play a true-lie game.** Describe yourself to a partner. **Student A:** Say two true sentences and one lie. **Student B:** Guess the lie. Take turns.

I can paint. I can sing. I can speak Swahili.

Number 3 is a lie! You can't speak Swahili!

Wrong! I can speak Swahili, but I can't sing.

The Real World

Superhumans!

Superhumans are people who have real-life super powers! Look at the people on this page. These people can do amazing things!

Daniel Kish

A **Look at the photos.** What do you think these people can do? Choose the correct answers.

1. Daniel Kish can ride a bicycle (**without seeing / as fast as a motorbike**).

2. Isao Machii can (**do magic tricks with fruit / cut fruit with his sword**).

3. Kevin Richardson can (**teach lions circus tricks / live with dangerous animals**).

B 🎧2–05 **Listen.** Circle **T** for True or **F** for False.

1. Daniel Kish can swim.   **T**   **F**

2. Kish was in a TV show.   **T**   **F**

3. Isao Machii can cut a tennis ball   **T**   **F**
   traveling as fast as a plane.

4. Kevin Richardson is also   **T**   **F**
   called the "Lion Talker."

Discussion. Which superhuman power do you want to have? Why?

Isao Machii

Kevin Richardson

Pronunciation

Can and *can't*

A 🎧2–06 **Listen and repeat.**

1. can, I can sing.   2. can't, I can't play the piano.

B 🎧2–07 **Listen.** Do you hear *can* or *can't*? Circle the correct word.

1. can	can't	2. can	can't	3. can	can't
4. can	can't	5. can	can't	6. can	can't

C **Work with a partner.** Take turns to read these sentences.

1. I can paint.   4. He can't speak Chinese.
2. I can't sing.   5. She can speak French.
3. I can surf.   6. They can't play tennis.

DO YOU KNOW?

This dog can walk on his paws. Do you think this picture is real?
a. Yes
b. No

Communication

Interview your classmates. Find out what they can or can't do.

Name: _____

1. Sing a song in English.
2. Name five English-speaking countries.
3. Count backwards from 20 to 0 in 20 seconds.
4. Say your phone number forwards and backwards.
5. Say the months of the year in ten seconds.
6. Roll your tongue.
7. _____.
8. _____.

Can you roll your tongue?

Yes, I can.

Kanzi eats food from a pan

Reading

A **Read the article quickly.** What's special about Kanzi?

    a. He can write.

    b. He can speak English.

    c. He can communicate with humans.

B **Circle all the things Kanzi can do.**

C **Read again.** Where does Kanzi live?

ANIMAL SMARTS

🎧 2–08

This is Kanzi, a bonobo chimpanzee. Bonobo chimpanzees are from Africa. There are only about 10,000 to 50,000 bonobos in the world today.

Kanzi lives in a zoo in the United States. He is very smart. He can
5 communicate with humans.

Kanzi can understand about 3,000 English words. He can't speak, but he can use the computer to say about 500 words. He points to pictures on a computer to say these words. He uses between 30 and 40 words every day.

10 Kanzi can also make a fire and cook marshmallows. He knows that fires are hot. Kanzi can't sing, but he can play the piano. Kanzi teaches his son Teco. Now Teco can use a computer, just like Kanzi.

Comprehension

A **Answer the questions about *Animal Smarts*.**

1. `Main Idea` What is the article about?

   a. a smart animal   b. bonobo chimpanzees   c. a zoo in the United States

2. `Detail` Where are Bonobo chimpanzees from?

   a. Africa   b. Europe   c. Asia

3. `Vocabulary` The word "understand" means _____ . (line 6)

   a. say   b. use   c. know the meaning of

4. `Inference` How does Kanzi communicate what he wants?

   a. by pointing to pictures   b. by writing words   c. by making sounds

5. `Detail` According to the article, Kanzi's son Teco can _____ .

   a. make a fire   b. use a computer   c. play the piano

B **Complete the chart.** According to the article, what can Kanzi do?

Kanzi can . . .	Kanzi can't . . .
understand 3,000 English words	

C **Talk with a partner.** Do you know any other smart animals? What can they do?

Writing

Write a short report about someone you know. Describe what they can and can't do.

My friend Lucy is friendly and very smart. She can't sing, but she can play the piano. She can surf, but she can't do a handstand.

Contact Juggling

BEFORE YOU WATCH

Circle the correct answer. Contact jugglers can _____.

a. roll balls on their bodies

b. play the piano and juggle

c. cut balls with their fingers

WHILE YOU WATCH

A **Check your answer to the Before You Watch question.**

B **Watch the video again.** Circle **T** for True or **F** for False.

1. Okotanpe works in Seoul, Korea.	T	F
2. Contact jugglers use balls made of glass.	T	F
3. The balls look like soap bubbles.	T	F
4. Contact juggling is very easy.	T	F
5. Okotanpe practices for several hours a day.	T	F
6. Okotanpe can also dance and do magic tricks.	T	F

AFTER YOU WATCH

Talk with a partner. What facts about contact juggling are interesting? Do you think contact juggling is fun?

A juggler practices contact juggling

HOW MUCH IS THIS
T-SHIRT?

Preview

A 🎧 2–09 **Listen.** Number the items the teenagers want to buy in the order you hear them (1–5).

backpack	T-shirt	shoes	hat	headphones
_____	_____	_____	_____	_____

B 🎧 2–09 **Listen again.** Match the item to its description.

ITEM			DESCRIPTION
1. backpack	○	○	a. red and black
2. T-shirt	○	○	b. large
3. shoes	○	○	c. small
4. hat	○	○	d. white
5. headphones	○	○	e. brown

C **Talk with a partner.** Do you like to shop? What's your favorite store?

> Where do you like to shop?

> I like to shop in the mall near my house.

A clothing shop in Vienna, Austria

Language Focus

A 🎧 2-10 **Listen and read.** Then repeat the conversation and replace the words in **blue**.

B **Practice with a partner.** Replace any words to make your own conversation.

REAL ENGLISH Excuse me.

🎧 2-11

TALKING ABOUT PRICES		
How much is this T-shirt? **How much are** those sneakers?	It's cheap. It's only $20. They're $50.	
I'd like that T-shirt, please.	Here you are. / Here you go.	I'd = I would
Would you like this baseball cap? **Would you like to see** these sneakers?	Yes, please. / No, thanks. **I'd like** that one. No, thanks. **I'd like to see** those ones, please.	

C 🎧 2–12 **Complete the conversation.** Then listen and check your answers.

1. A: _____ this wallet?

   B: _____ $12.

2. A: _____ that watch?

   B: _____ $50.

3. A: _____ this cap?

   B: _____ cheap.

   _____ $10.

4. A: _____ those books?

   B: _____ $15.

D 🎧 2–13 **Complete the conversation.** Listen and check your answers. Then practice the conversation with a partner.

Buyer: Excuse me, can I see that sweatshirt, please?

Seller: (1) _____ you (2) _____ to see the blue one?

Buyer: No, (3) I'_____ (4) _____ to see the red one, please.

Seller: Here you go. It's $30.

Buyer: Hmm, it's too expensive. (5) _____ is the blue one?

Seller: It's $25.

Buyer: OK, great. (6) I'_____ (7) _____ the blue one, please.

E **Work in pairs.** You are at a store. **Student A:** You are a customer. **Student B:** You are a store assistant. Put some personal items on your desk, and try to buy or sell them.

Excuse me, can I see that phone, please?

Sure, here you are.

How much is it?

It's $20. Would you like to buy it?

Yes, please. / No, thanks.

The Real World

Haggling

To *haggle* means to discuss the price of something. The buyer and seller try to agree on a good price. People don't usually haggle in stores, but they sometimes haggle in markets.

A 🎧 2-14 **Guess the rules of haggling.** Circle **T** for True or **F** for False. Listen and check.

1. Learn the real price before you buy.   **T   F**

2. Be very friendly.   **T   F**

3. The first price is usually the best.   **T   F**

4. Show the seller you're interested.   **T   F**

5. Walk away if you don't like the price.   **T   F**

6. It's important to be nice.   **T   F**

B 🎧 2-15 **Guess.** Who do you think says each sentence? Circle **B** for Buyer or **S** for Seller. Then put the sentences in the correct order. Listen and check your answers.

__1__ "Excuse me, can I see that box, please?"   **B   S**

____ "No, that's too expensive. How about $30?"   **B   S**

____ "Here you go. It's $50. Would you like to buy it?"   **B   S**

____ "Ok, you can have it for $35."   **B   S**

____ "That's still too expensive."   **B   S**

____ "That's too cheap. I can sell it for $40."   **B   S**

Discussion. Do you think haggling is easy? Use the sentences above to make your own conversation.

Pronunciation
Prices

A 🎧 2–16 **Listen and repeat the prices.**

1. a. $2.99   b. $2.99
2. a. $14.10   b. $14.10

B 🎧 2–17 **Listen and circle the prices you hear.**

1. $100	$200	4. $207.90	$27.90
2. $20.95	$29.75	5. $56.50	$50.60
3. $10.25	$10.35	6. $6.10	$64.10

C **Work with a partner.** Take turns to read the prices in **B**.

DO YOU KNOW?

Which country uses pesos?
a. Canada
b. Mexico
c. The United States

Communication

Complete the chart. Look at the picture on page 81. Choose **three items** you want to buy. Write them in the chart. Then ask three students for their prices. Haggle to get cheap prices. Then talk to your class. Whose things are cheap? Whose are expensive?

ITEM	STUDENT A	STUDENT B	STUDENT C
1.			
2.			
3.			

Can I see that key ring, please?

Sure.

How much is it?

It's $4.

No, that's too expensive. How about $3?

Reading

A **Look at the photo and the title.** How is this mall different from other malls?

B **Read the article quickly.** <u>Underline</u> the places you can go to in this mall.

C **Read again.** What country is Dubai in?

SKIING IN A SHOPPING MALL?

🎧 2–18

Dubai is a city in the United Arab Emirates. Around two million people live there. The Mall of the Emirates is the second largest mall in Dubai. Over 36 million visitors visit this mall every year.

The mall is very big. It's also very famous, and has over 25 awards.
5 You can spend the whole day here. It has everything! You can go shopping. You can eat. You can watch a movie or see a play here, too. The Mall of the Emirates has about 500 stores: clothing stores, bookstores, and electronic stores. There are more than 85 restaurants and cafés, two hotels, a movie theater with 14 screens, and a theater.
10 It even has a ski slope. It's true—you can ski in the desert! It's hot in Dubai, but it's very cold on the ski slope.

Comprehension

A) Answer the questions about *Skiing in a Shopping Mall?*

1. Main Idea What is another title for the article?

   a. An Amazing Mall   b. A Strange Ski Slope   c. A Beautiful Country

2. Vocabulary The word "famous" means _____ . (line 4)

   a. full of people   b. different   c. well-known

3. Inference "You can spend the whole day here" means you can _____ . (line 5)

   a. do a lot of things   b. buy a lot of things   c. spend a lot of money

4. Detail How many stores does the mall have?

   a. about 350   b. about 400   c. about 500

5. Inference "You can ski in the desert!" means you can ski _____ . (line 10)

   a. on the sand   b. in cold weather   c. in a desert country

B) Match the numbers to the correct answers.

1.   2 ◯   ◯ a. restaurants and cafés

2. 14 ◯   ◯ b. awards

3. 25 ◯   ◯ c. hotels

4. 85 ◯   ◯ d. movie screens

5. 500 ◯   ◯ e. stores

C) CRITICAL THINKING Talk with a partner. Would you like to go to Dubai's Mall of the Emirates? What would you like to do there?

Writing

Write a blog post. Describe your favorite market, mall, or store.

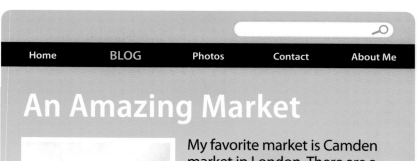

Home   BLOG   Photos   Contact   About Me

An Amazing Market

My favorite market is Camden market in London. There are a lot of street markets, but this one is amazing! You can buy cool things there. People sell T-shirts, baseball caps, and posters. They sell delicious food from a lot of countries, too. I love the fruit juices.

A Moroccan Market

Shops in Fez

BEFORE YOU WATCH

Look at the photo and read the title. What do you think you can buy in a Moroccan market? Make a list.

_____

WHILE YOU WATCH

A **Check.** What items on your list did you see?

B **Watch the video again.** Circle the correct answer.

1. The marketplace in Fez is also called a _____.

   a. fair   b. souk

2. If you are shopping in the market, you need to _____.

   a. haggle   b. get up early

3. What does the tourist want to buy?

   a. a bracelet   b. earrings

4. What price did the seller first ask for?

   a. 140 dirhams   b. 225 dirhams

5. What price does the tourist pay?

   a. 130 dirhams   b. 190 dirhams

AFTER YOU WATCH

Talk with a partner. Do you think the tourist haggles well? How is this market similar to or different from markets where you live?

WHAT ARE YOU
DOING?

**Visitors playing a computer
game during a games fair**

Preview

A 🎧 2–19 **Listen.** Number what each person is doing in the order you hear them (1–6).

📷	✉️	📞	💬	🎮	📱
taking a photo	checking email	calling a friend	chatting	playing a game	texting
____	____	____	____	____	_1_

B **How techie are you?** Complete the survey on page 132 and see your results.

C **Talk with a partner.** Compare your results.

> I send seven or more texts in a day.

> Really? I only send three or four texts!

Language Focus

A 🎧 2–20 **Listen and read.** Then repeat the conversation and replace the words in **blue**.

REAL ENGLISH just

B **Practice with a partner.** Replace any words to make your own conversation.

🎧 2–21

TALKING ABOUT WHAT SOMEONE IS DOING	
What **are** you **doing**?	I'm **texting**.
What's he **doing**?	He's **checking** his **email**.
Are they **watching** a movie? **Is** she **listening** to music? Who **are** you **chatting** with?	**Yes**, they **are**. / **No**, they're **not**. **Yes**, she **is**. / **No**, she's **not**. I'm **chatting** with a friend.

C Complete the questions. Then match the questions to the correct answers.

1. ____Are____ you ___using___ this computer? (*use*) ○   ○ She's chatting with a friend.

2. Who _____ Kelly _____ with? (*chat*) ○   ○ He's playing a video game.

3. _____ she _____ Anna? (*text*) ○   ○ No, she isn't.

4. _____ they _____ a movie? (*watch*) ○   ○ Yes, I am. I'm checking my email.

5. What _____ Tom _____? (*do*) ○   ○ Yes, they are.

D 🎧 2–22 **Complete the conversation.** Use the correct form of the words from the box. Listen and check your answers.

> chat   do   play   listen   study

Sarah: Hey Anna, what (1) _____ you _____? (2) _____ you _____ for the test?

Anna: No I'm not! (3) I'_____ _____ a game on my computer. What about you?

Sarah: (4) I'_____ just _____ with friends and listening to some music.

Anna: Really? What (5) _____ you _____ to?

Sarah: Beyoncé. She's my favorite singer!

E **Play charades in two teams.**
Team A: Think of an action and act it out.
Team B: Guess what Team A is doing. You have three chances. Take turns.

Are you playing a game?

Yes, I am!

The Real World

Robots and Microrobots

Robert Wood is a National Geographic Explorer. He is also an electrical engineer. He makes many different types of robots—from robots that fly to robots you can wear. He is now working on making new robots at Harvard University.

A **Look at the photo below and the caption.** What is a "microrobot"?

a. a small robot   b. a flying robot   c. a robot that looks like a bee

B 🎧 2–23 **Listen to the article about Robert Wood.** Then answer the following questions.

1. Wood is also a (**professor** / **student**).

2. RoboBees are the size of a (**bird** / **fly**).

3. RoboBees can (**go into dangerous places** / **help in cooking food**).

4. Millibots are some of the (**fastest** / **smallest**) robots in the world.

Microrobots called Robobees

Discussion. What else do you think RoboBees can help in doing?

Pronunciation

Intonation in *Wh-* questions and *yes/no* questions

A 🎧 2–24 **Listen to the intonation.** Listen again and repeat.

1. What are you doing?   2. Are you studying?

B 🎧 2–25 **Listen to the questions.** Circle the correct intonation.

1. a. Are they watching a movie?   b. Are they watching a movie?
2. a. Do you read blogs?   b. Do you read blogs?
3. a. What's she writing?   b. What's she writing?
4. a. Are you texting him now?   b. Are you texting him now?
5. a. Do you like movies?   b. Do you like movies?
6. a. What game are you playing?   b. What game are you playing?

C **Work with a partner.** Take turns to ask questions in **B**.

DO YOU KNOW?

What makes more money every year?

a. Hollywood movies
b. Video games

Communication

Find the differences. Student A: Look at the picture below. **Student B:** Look at the picture on page 133. Ask and answer questions about the pictures.

In my picture Anna is chatting with Maria.

In my picture Anna is using a computer.

Julie   Maria   Anna   Tom

Manuela

Natalie

Jake   David

Reading

A **Look at the photo and scan the article.** Who made Leon's new hand? Check (✓) the correct answer.

◯ Leon's dad   ◯ a doctor   ◯ an engineer

B **Read the title.** What do you think the title means?

C **Read quickly.** Underline the things that 3D printers can make.

HOW 3D PRINTERS ARE CHANGING LIVES

🎧 2–26

Leon McCarthy has no fingers on his left hand, so his dad made a new hand on a 3D printer at home. His new low-cost hand is changing his life. Now he can pick up things. He can also throw a ball, and ride a bike—with both hands!

5 **What is a 3D printer?**

A 3D printer uses plastic to print 3D objects. It can make hands, fingers, or feet at a cheap price. It can make jewelry, toys, and sunglasses, too! 3D printers are becoming very popular because they can make almost everything! Some designers are even using 3D
10 printers to print food and houses! Schools are also using 3D printers to teach students design.

How does a 3D printer work?

There are three main steps in 3D printing. First, a person uses software or a scanner to design an object. Then, the printer checks
15 the object's shape and size. Finally, the printer uses plastic to print the object.

Leon McCarthy using
his new plastic hand

Comprehension

A Answer the questions about *How 3D Printers Are Changing Lives.*

1. **Main Idea** The article is mainly about how 3D printers _____.

   a. are helping people   b. design objects   c. print objects

2. **Vocabulary** "Low cost" means _____. (line 2)

   a. made of plastic   b. 3D   c. not very expensive

3. **Detail** What does a 3D printer usually make an object from?

   a. plastic   b. wood   c. metal

4. **Reference** In line 8, what does "they" mean?

   a. designers   b. 3D printers   c. schools

5. **Detail** A person uses _____ to design an object.

   a. a pencil   b. plastic   c. software or a scanner

> **IDIOM**
>
> "Pushing someone's buttons" means _____.
>
> a. making them angry
> b. teaching them something

B **Complete the sentences.** Write the steps of how a 3D printer makes an object.

> **Step 1:** A person uses software or scanner to
> _____

> **Step 2:** The printer checks the object's
> _____

> **Step 3:** Printer uses plastic to
> _____

C **CRITICAL THINKING** **Talk with a partner.** In what other ways do you think 3D printers can change lives?

Writing

Write a short paragraph about technology. What apps are you and your friends using at the moment?

> These days, I'm using different apps to stay in touch with my friends. I can use these apps to share photos and chat with them.
>
> I'm using one app to send instant messages to my friends. I'm using a different app to share my photos. I'm also sharing a lot of videos with them.
>
> My friends and I are also playing lots of games. We usually play games after finishing our homework!

A New Photographer

ABOUT THE VIDEO

A photographer shows us how to take close-up photographs of lions.

BEFORE YOU WATCH

Circle the correct answer. Who do you think took the photo of the lions below?

a. a photographer   b. a remote-controlled car   c. an animal

WHILE YOU WATCH

A **Check your answer to the Before You Watch question.**

B **Watch the video again.** Complete the information below using the words in the labels.

buggy

remote control

camera

Chris McLennan puts the _____ in a small car. This small car is also called a _____. McLennan is using a _____ to control the car. The car is taking photographs of lions in the wild.

AFTER YOU WATCH

Talk with a partner. Describe the car to a partner. If you had a car like this, what photographs would you take?

Lions in Botswana

WHAT'S THE WEATHER LIKE?

A rainy street in
Kolkata, India

Preview

A 🎧 2–27 **Listen.** Number the weather conditions in the order you hear them (1–4).

				hot
It's rainy.	It's sunny.	It's windy.	It's stormy.	warm
_____	_____	_____	_____	cool
				cold

B 🎧 2–28 **Listen and complete the chart.** What's the weather like?

	RAINY	SUNNY	WINDY	STORMY	WARM	HOT	COOL	COLD
Shanghai	✓							
Cape Town								
Rio de Janeiro								
Stockholm								

C **Talk with a partner.** What's the weather like today? What kind of weather do you like?

> Today, the weather is cold. I like the weather to be warm and sunny.

Language Focus

A 🎧 2–29 **Listen and read.** Then repeat the conversation and replace the words in **blue**.

B **Practice with a partner.** Replace any words to make your own conversation.

1 Hey, Stig. What's the weather like in Sweden today?

It's **snowy**. It's always **snowy** in winter here.

cold
icy

2 Oh! So, what are you doing now?

I'm doing something **fun**!

exciting
interesting

3 Cool! Are you **at home**?

No, I'm not!

indoors
in school

4 Come on, Stig! Tell me what you're doing!

I'm snowboarding!

🎧 2–30

TALKING ABOUT WEATHER

What's the weather **like** today? **What's** the weather **like** in summer? **What's** the weather **like** in April?	**It's** cold. **It's** always dry and hot. **It's** usually warm, but it's sometimes rainy.
Is it usually cold in winter?	Yes, **it is**. No, **it isn't**.
How hot **is** it?	**It's** (about) 30 degrees. (30°) **It's** (about) minus 12 degrees. (-12°)

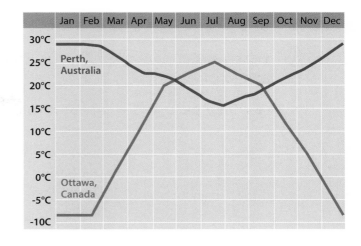

C 🎧 2–31 **Look at the weather chart.** Complete the conversation. Listen and check your answers. Then practice with a partner.

Hunter: What's the weather like where you live?

Sarah: Well, in Perth, it's always 1. (**hot** / **cold**) in January and February. That's the 2. (**summer** / **autumn**) here.

Hunter: Really? So when is it winter in Australia?

Sarah: Well, winter is from 3. (**June to September** / **November to January**).

Hunter: In Ottawa, winter is from 4. (**November to March** / **October to December**). It's always really 5. (**cold** / **cool**). Winters are long and snowy.

Sarah: Is it hot in the summer?

Hunter: Well, it's sometimes hot, but it's usually 6. (**warm and sunny** / **cool and dry**).

D **What's the weather like where you live?** Answer the questions. Discuss your answers with a partner.

1. What's the weather like in March?   _____.

2. What's the weather like in October?   _____.

3. How hot is it in summer?   _____.

4. Is it usually warm and sunny in August? _____.

5. What's the weather like in spring?   _____.

E **What's the weather like in South Africa today? Student A:** Look at the weather map below. **Student B:** Turn to page 133. Ask and answer questions to complete the temperatures and weather conditions on your map.

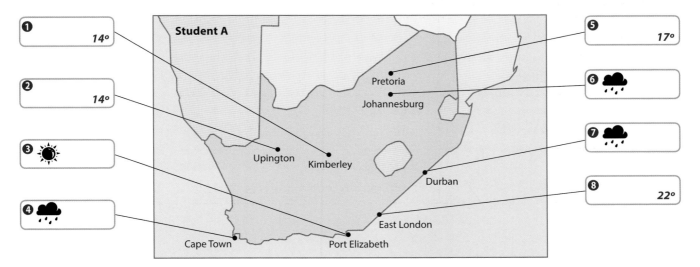

The Real World

Unusual Weather

Weather is sometimes very strange. Here are some amazing facts about unusual weather.

This is a tornado. A tornado is a kind of _____ with very strong winds.

A **Look at the photos.** Complete the captions with the words from the box.

> storm   ice
> tornadoes   tennis

B 🎧 2–32 **Listen to facts about the weather.** Circle **T** for True or **F** for False.

1. Tornadoes are always the same color.   **T**   **F**
2. Tornadoes can pick up houses and move them.   **T**   **F**
3. Another word for tornadoes is "spinners."   **T**   **F**
4. Hailstones sometimes have things inside them.   **T**   **F**

Discussion. What weather fact on this page do you think is the most interesting? Why?

These hailstones are made of _____. Hailstones are cold and hard. Some hailstones are really big, like _____ balls.

_____ can pick up small animals like frogs. Then it can rain frogs!

Pronunciation
Final -y sound

A 🎧 2-33 **Listen and repeat.**

1. wind, windy
2. sun, sunny

B 🎧 2-34 **Listen.** Circle the word you hear.

1. ice   icy   4. cloud   cloudy
2. snow   snowy   5. rain   rainy
3. storm   stormy   6. wind   windy

C **Work with a partner.** Take turns to read the words in **B**.

Communication

Weather report. In pairs, complete the chart below for five cities of your choice.
Student A: You are the TV presenter. **Student B:** You are the weather reporter. Present the report to your class.

CITY	TEMPERATURE	WEATHER
London	21°C	warm and sunny
1.		
2.		
3.		
4.		
5.		

What's the weather like in London, Jennifer?

Today, the weather in London is warm and sunny. The temperature is 21 degrees Celsius.

Roger Hill in front
of a tornado

Reading

A **Look at the photo and read the caption.** Who do you think Roger Hill is?

   a. a photographer

   b. a weather reporter

   c. a TV reporter

B **Read the title.** What do you think storm chasers do?

C **Read the article quickly.** Underline the words that mean the opposite of "away."

STORM CHASER

🎧 2–35

Most people run away from tornadoes, but Roger Hill runs toward them. He is a "storm chaser." He takes photos of storms. He has photos of more than 650 tornadoes!

Hill runs a company called Silver Lining Tours. His company organizes
5 trips for people who want to see tornadoes. He spends about four months every year traveling. He travels all over the United States looking for tornadoes. He finds them by checking the Internet for weather information. When he finds a storm, he starts driving toward it. His company's cars have special equipment to help him follow the
10 storms.

Whenever he's chasing and photographing tornadoes, Hill knows he needs to be safe. He says you can get close to a tornado and take a picture. However, if you make a mistake, it can kill you. So in a way, it's like a photographer trying to take photos of grizzly bears. Before
15 taking a photograph you need to be ready and to have an escape route. Safety is really important!

Comprehension

A **Answer the questions about *Storm Chaser*.**

1. Main Idea The article is mainly about _____ .

   a. a person who chases storms

   b. how storms form into tornadoes

   c. how to stay safe from storms

2. Reference In line 7, what does "them" mean?

   a. people   b. tornadoes   c. tours

3. Inference Tornadoes and grizzly bears are both _____ .

   a. fast   b. dangerous   c. difficult to find

4. Vocabulary What is an "escape route"? (lines 15–16)

   a. a fast car   b. a hiding place   c. a way of getting away

5. Detail Hill says _____ is really important.

   a. safety   b. time   c. weather information

B **Read the article again.** Put the sentences in order from 1 to 4.

   1. _____   2. _____   3. _____   4. _____

   a. Hill finds the storm.   b. Hill photographs the storm.

   c. Hill checks his escape route.   d. Hill starts driving toward the storm.

C **CRITICAL THINKING** Do you think Roger Hill's job sounds exciting or scary?

Writing

Write a postcard. Imagine you are on vacation. Tell a friend where you are and what the weather is like.

Hi Melanie!

I'm on an island near Hawaii! It's very beautiful! The weather is really nice. The temperature is around 30 degrees. It's usually sunny during the day. The waves are amazing, and I can surf almost every day.

The problem is that it's raining today and I don't know what to do! I'm waiting for it to be sunny again!

Wish you were here,

Alberto

POST OFFICE
POSTAGE
OFFICE

Tornado Chasers

ABOUT THE VIDEO
See how scientists chase tornadoes.

BEFORE YOU WATCH

Guess. Complete the advice about tornadoes.

When there is a tornado:

a. it's a (**good** / **bad**) idea to hide in the basement.

b. it's a (**good** / **bad**) idea to hide under a table.

c. it's a (**good** / **bad**) idea to stay near windows.

WHILE YOU WATCH

A **Check your answers to the Before You Watch question.**

B **Watch the video again.** Circle **T** for True or **F** for False.

1. There are more than 8,000 tornadoes in the United States every year.   **T**   **F**

2. Many tornadoes take place in an area called "Twister alley."   **T**   **F**

3. Scientists drive cars with special equipment to study tornadoes.   **T**   **F**

4. Scientists study tornadoes to help keep people safe.   **T**   **F**

AFTER YOU WATCH

Talk with a partner. Why do you think storm chasers do such dangerous work? Would you want to be a storm chaser?

Storm chaser Brad Mack photographing a thunderstorm supercell in Graham, U.S.A.

I WENT TO AUSTRALIA!

Preview

A 🎧2-36 **Listen to the conversation.** Circle **T** for True or **F** for False.

1. Rena went to Melbourne.   T   F

2. It was cold and rainy.   T   F

3. She went with her friends.   T   F

4. She had a good time.   T   F

B 🎧2-37 **Listen.** What did Rena do in Australia? Circle the correct answers.

"We did a lot of exciting things. On our first day we went to the mountains. We
1. (**cycled** / **trekked**) all the way to the top. We spent the next day 2. (**swimming** /
surfing) at the beach. There are a lot of amazing 3. (**restaurants** / **cafés**) in Melbourne.
We had some really interesting food. We also went to see a few 4. (**museums** /
art galleries). There was so much to do!"

C **Talk with a partner.** What places do you like to visit in your country? Why?

> I like to visit Okinawa. I like it because it has a lot of beautiful beaches.

A surfer at Remarkable Caves,
Tasmania, Australia

Language Focus

A 🎧 2-38 **Listen and read.** Then repeat the conversation and replace the words in blue.

REAL ENGLISH That sounds great!

B **Practice with a partner.** Replace any words to make your own conversation.

1 How was your **vacation**?

Well, it was good and bad.

adventure trip

2 Why's that?

Well, my **dad** got us air tickets to London. My family loves England.

brother
grandfather

3 OK . . . so what did you do?

We went to a **museum**. We saw the river. We had fun.

restaurant
mall

4 That sounds **great**! So what was the problem?

He got air tickets to London, Canada, not London, England! We went to the wrong country!

amazing
good

🎧 2-39

TALKING ABOUT PAST EVENTS	
How **was** your vacation? How **were** the beaches?	It **was** amazing! They **were** beautiful!
What **did** you **do**?	I **went** to the beach. I **ate** a lot of good food. I **stayed** at home. I **saw** a beautiful museum.
Did you **go** surfing?	Yes, I **did**. / No, I **didn't**.
When **did** you **go**?	I went **last summer** / **last week** / **last year**.

C 🎧2-40 **Complete the conversation.** Circle the correct words. Then listen and check your answers.

Jasmine: How 1. (**was** / **is**) your weekend, Mina?

Mina: It 2. (**was** / **were**) great.

Jasmine: What did you 3. (**do** / **did**)?

Mina: I 4. (**go** / **went**) to the beach.

Jasmine: Really? What 5. (**did** / **do**) you 6. (**did** / **do**) there?

Mina: Well, I 7. (**went** / **was**) surfing. It 8. (**was** / **had**) a lot of fun.

Jasmine: 9. (**Did** / **do**) you go with your parents?

Mina: No, I 10. (**went** / **go**) with my cousins.

IDIOM

Do you like to travel a lot? That means you have the ____ .

a. travel bug
b. visit worm

D **Complete the conversation.**   Use the correct form of the words.

Last year I (1) _____ (**go**) to France. It (2) _____ (**be**) a great trip.
I (3) _____ (**do**) a lot of shopping. I also went to a museum and (4) _____ (**see**)
the Eiffel Tower. I (5) _____ (**go**) with my parents. But my brother (6) _____
(**stay**) at home.

E **Play a game.** Get into small groups. Take turns to add a sentence to the following story.

Story: Yesterday I went to the park . . .

I saw an old woman . . .

. . . She was very angry.

The Real World

Australian Adventure

Andrew Evans is a National Geographic Explorer. He travels all over the world and writes about his adventures. In 2010, Evans visited Australia. Find out more about his trip.

A 🎧 **2–41** **Listen.** Match the questions to the places.

1. Where did Evans go first? ○   ○ a. Sydney

2. Where did he go diving? ○   ○ b. Perth

3. Where did he celebrate Australia Day? ○   ○ c. Cairns

4. Where did he see a kangaroo? ○   ○ d. Melbourne

B 🎧 **2–42** **Listen.** What did Evans do in Australia? Circle the correct answers.

Andrew Evans stayed in 1. (**Melbourne** / **Australia**) for more than two months. He visited almost every 2. (**state** / **museum**) in the country and traveled almost 30,000 kilometers! He loved the country and the 3. (**people** / **landscape**). He thinks Australia is a great place. He was really happy he went there and hopes to 4. (**go there again** / **live there**) one day.

Discussion. Do you want to go to Australia? What do you want to do there?

Pronunciation
Regular past tense verb endings: -ed endings

A 🎧 2–43 **Listen and repeat.**

1. They stay<u>ed</u> in a great place. /d/
2. I check<u>ed</u> my emails in the hotel. /t/
3. We visit<u>ed</u> a museum. /id/

B 🎧 2–44 **Listen.** Circle the correct sounds.

1. We watched a movie on the airplane. /d/ /t/ /id/
2. He invited me to a picnic. /d/ /t/ /id/
3. She shared her photos. /d/ /t/ /id/
4. I liked Australia. /d/ /t/ /id/
5. We wanted to go to England. /d/ /t/ /id/
6. They hiked in the mountains. /d/ /t/ /id/

C **Work with a partner.** Take turns to read the sentences in **B**.

DO YOU KNOW?

Which country has the most tourists every year?
a. The United States
b. France

Communication

Create a story. Pair A: Tell Pair B a story about a trip you or your partner went on. Include three statements that are not true. **Pair B:** Guess the statements that are not true. Take turns.

Last year I went to Australia for a week. I saw a kangaroo and a Tasmanian devil . . .

You didn't go to Australia last year! You went this year, and you didn't see a Tasmanian devil . . .

Reading

A **Read the article quickly.** Choose a different title.

    a. How to Travel Around the World

    b. A Short Adventure in Africa

    c. Around the World in 12 Months

B **Underline all the places the Davis family visited.**

C **Read again.** Which country is the Davis family from? _____

TRAVELERS of THE YEAR

🎧 2–45

In 2011, Canadian travel writer Heather Greenwood Davis and her husband, Ike, went on an adventure. They took their two sons—Ethan and Cameron—out of school, and went on a round-the-world trip.

5 In total, the Davis family spent 12 months on the road and went to 29 countries. They saw amazing birds in the Galápagos islands, climbed volcanoes, and helped at a children's hospital in China. They even came close to a huge bear in Canada. They went to beautiful temples in Cambodia. They also traveled into the rain forests of
10 Thailand and saw really big Asian elephants.

While they traveled, they wrote many travel blog posts. They also took lots of photos.

Now back home in Canada, Heather says that her family learned many things. They learned that the world is a beautiful place full of
15 amazing people. Traveling made her see how we are all like each other. We can all make friends everywhere we go.

The Davis family, National
Geographic travelers of the year

Comprehension

A **Answer the questions about *Travelers of the Year*.**

1. Main Idea   The article is about _____ .

   a. a school trip   b. a travel blog   c. an adventure holiday

2. Vocabulary   The Davis family spent 12 months "on the road." This means they spent 12 months _____ . (line 5)

   a. traveling   b. driving   c. trekking

3. Detail   In Cambodia, the family visited _____ .

   a. beaches   b. mountains   c. temples

4. Detail   What did they see in Thailand?

   a. a bear   b. elephants   c. amazing birds

5. Paraphrase   In line 15, "we are all like each other" means _____ .

   a. we are all friendly   b. we are all amazing   c. we all are the same

B **Complete the chart.** What can travelers do in these places? Use information from the article and then add your own ideas.

Galápagos Islands	Cambodia	Thailand	Your Country
See amazing birds			

C **CRITICAL THINKING**   **Talk with a partner.** Do you want to go on an around-the-world trip? Why? Where do you want to go?

Writing

Write a travel blog. Describe what you saw and did.

| Home | BLOG | Photos | Contact | About Me |

I'm on vacation in New Zealand with my family.

My family and I went to a redwood forest on the North Island. The redwood trees were really big. We also saw the beautiful city of Christchurch on the South Island.

Yesterday, we climbed a mountain. I was really tired when we reached our hotel but we had a lot of fun!

An Amazing Journey

ABOUT THE VIDEO

Andrew Evans travels to ten countries in 24 days.

BEFORE YOU WATCH

Match the places to the events. Look at the map below. What do you think Andrew Evans did in each of the places?

1. Maldives ○
2. Nepal ○
3. Botswana ○

○ a. saw mountains
○ b. saw lions
○ c. dived

WHILE YOU WATCH

A Check your answers to the Before You Watch question.

B Watch the video again. Draw Evans' journey on the map below.

Andrew Evans holds up the National Geographic flag at the Uyuni Salt Flat, Bolivia.

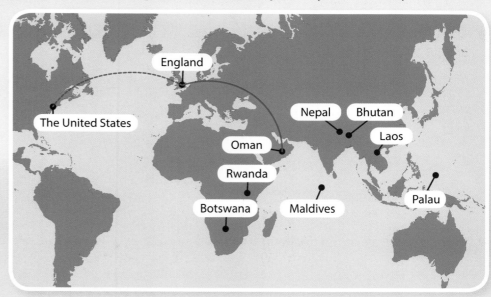

England

The United States

Nepal   Bhutan

Laos

Oman

Rwanda

Botswana   Maldives

Palau

AFTER YOU WATCH

Talk with a partner. Which country in the video do you want to visit? Tell a partner about your last vacation.

WHAT DO YOU USUALLY DO FOR NEW YEAR'S?

People celebrating the Yee Peng festival in Chiang Mai, Thailand

An Amazing Journey

BEFORE YOU WATCH

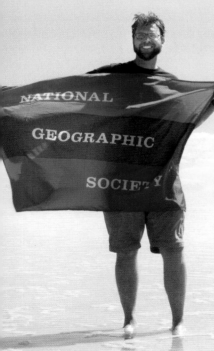

Preview

A 🎧 2–46 **Listen.** Match the teenagers to the occasions they celebrate.

1. Maria ○   ○ a. goes to a festival. He watches a _____.

2. Yang ○   ○ b celebrates Chinese New Year. He watches the _____.

3. Philippe ○   ○ c. celebrates her birthday. She has a _____.

4. Aditi ○   ○ d. celebrates New Year. She puts up _____.

5. Chrystie ○   ○ e. celebrates Diwali. She eats _____.

B 🎧 2–46 **Listen again.** Complete the sentences (1–5) in **A**. Use the words below.

fireworks   party   decorations   special food   parade

C **Talk with a partner.** How do you celebrate your favorite festival?

> What's your favorite festival? How do you celebrate it?

Language Focus

A 🎧2–47 **Listen and read.** Then repeat the conversation and replace the words in blue.

B **Practice with a partner.** Replace any words to make your own conversation.

1. Hi Nadine! How was your weekend?
   It was **good**, thanks. (OK / great)

2. What did you do on Saturday?
   Um, I visited my **aunt and uncle**. (grandparents / cousins)

3. That's nice! What about yesterday?
   Yesterday . . . I went to a **night festival**. (barbecue / party)

4. And what are you doing now?
   Taking a nap . . . you woke me up! (Sleeping / Napping)

🎧2–48

TALKING ABOUT SPECIAL OCCASIONS	
I went to a festival **during** the holidays.	
What did you do **on** New Year's Eve? What did you do **in** summer?	We **went** to a party. I **visited** my family.
Did you go on vacation **for** Chinese New Year?	Yes, I did. No, I didn't. I **stayed** at home.

C 🎧 2-49 **Complete the conversation.** Use the words in the box. Listen and check.

> in   on   during

David: When's your birthday, Elisa?

Elisa: It was last month. It was (1) _____ July 10th.

David: Great! What did you do?

Elisa: Well, it was (2) _____ the summer holidays, so I went to Spain. When is your birthday, David?

David: Well, my birthday is (3) _____ winter. It's (4) _____ the winter holidays!

Elisa: Oh I remember! It's (5) _____ December 23rd. I came to your birthday party last year!

D **Complete the conversation.** Use the correct form of the words from the box.

> be   eat   open   do   visit   put   have   watch

For my birthday, I usually (1) _____ a party at home. I also (2) _____ special food. My aunt and uncle always (3) _____ my home. We all (4) _____ up decorations. Last year, we had a barbecue party and fireworks. We all (5) _____ the fireworks and ate some good food. Then we (6) _____ the cards and the presents. It (7) _____ great. I hope we can (8) _____ the same thing this year.

E **Play a game with a partner. Student A:** Imagine you had a party. **Student B:** Ask your partner questions and find out more information. Take turns.

When was your party?

It was on December 31st.

Was it a New Year's Eve party?

Incense sticks outside a temple on Chinese New Year, Malacca, Malaysia

Festivals
Around the World

Countries all around the world celebrate different types of festivals. People eat special food, dance, and have a good time. At festivals, people sometimes dress up in amazing costumes and put on brightly colored makeup. Festival costumes are sometimes strange, scary, or funny. Here are some unusual costumes from Europe.

A 🎧2–50 **Listen.** Number the costumes in the photos in the order you hear their descriptions.

B 🎧2–51 **Listen.** Circle **T** for True or **F** for False.

1. Festivals in Europe usually take place from the beginning of November.   **T**   **F**
2. In Portugal, people decorate trees during the Lazarim Carnival.   **T**   **F**
3. During the Lazarim Carnival, there are singing competitions.   **T**   **F**
4. In Spain, people have a festival to enjoy the last nights of summer.   **T**   **F**
5. People wear scary costumes during a carnival in Austria.   **T**   **F**

Discussion. Which festival on this page is your favorite? Why?

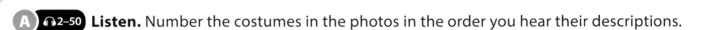

Pronunciation
Syllable stress

A 🎧 2–52 **Listen to the stressed syllables.** Repeat the words.

1. <u>bar</u>becue   2. deco<u>ra</u>tion

B 🎧 2–53 **Listen and underline the stressed syllable.**

1. festival   2. vacation   3. party   4. celebrate

5. around   6. summer   7. amazing   8. winter

C **Work with a partner.** Take turns reading the words in **B**.

Communication

Take a class survey. How did your classmates celebrate their birthdays last year? Ask questions and note the names. Then add more information.

FIND SOMEONE WHO . . .	NAME	MORE INFORMATION
. . . went out with friends.		
. . . spent time with his or her family.		
. . . watched a movie.		
. . . went somewhere interesting.		
. . . had a party.		

Hey, what did you do for your birthday last year?

I went out with friends.

Cool! Who did you go with?

Ming and Maya.

The Harbin Ice and Snow
Festival in China

Reading

A **Look at the photo and read the title.** When do you think this festival takes place? What do you think the weather is like?

B **Read quickly.** Underline the weather words.

C **Read again.** Where is the city of Harbin located?

HARBIN ICE
and SNOW FESTIVAL

🎧 2–54

Every year, on January 5th, the city of Harbin in northeast China changes into a winter wonderland. Tourists from all around the world come to visit this amazing ice and snow festival.

The festival started in 1963 and began as a winter party. The festival
5 usually lasts for one month. However, if the weather stays cold and dry, it goes on for a few more days. Temperatures are usually very cold. They can go down to -17°C.

Ice sculptors use different tools to carve the hard ice and snow. These sculptors display their work in two main areas. "Sun Island" has huge
10 snow sculptures of people and animals. "Ice and Snow World" has sculptures of buildings. At night, these buildings light up with brightly-colored lights.

Visitors can do a lot of other activities, such as skiing and ice sliding. They can also go swimming in the icy waters of the Songhua River.

15 The Harbin Ice and Snow Festival is very popular. Every year, hundreds of thousands of people visit the festival.

Comprehension

A Answer the questions about *Harbin Ice and Snow Festival.*

1. Main Idea This article is mainly about _____.

   a. a festival in China   b. a winter party   c. festivals around the world

2. Inference The festival continues for more than a month if the weather is _____.

   a. cold and wet   b. cold and dry   c. cold and sunny

3. Vocabulary People who make things from ice and snow are called _____.

   a. sculptures   b. monuments   c. sculptors

4. Vocabulary What does the word "display" mean? (line 9)

   a. carve   b. show   c. make

5. Detail Which activity is NOT mentioned in the article?

   a. skating   b. skiing   c. swimming

B Complete the word web.

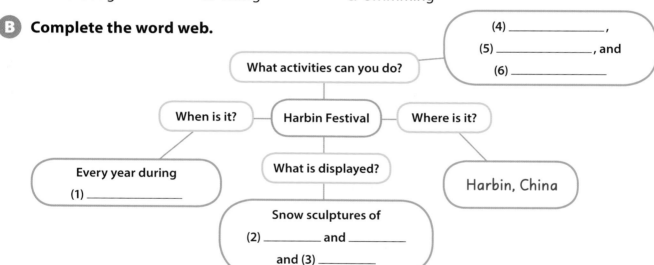

What activities can you do?
(4) _____ ,
(5) _____ , and
(6) _____

When is it?   Harbin Festival   Where is it?

Every year during
(1) _____

What is displayed?

Harbin, China

Snow sculptures of
(2) _____ and _____
and (3) _____

C CRITICAL THINKING **Talk with a partner.** Do you like festivals? Would you like to go to the Harbin Ice and Snow Festival?

Writing

Write a postcard.
Tell your friend
about a carnival.

Hi Yoko,

Greetings from Rio de Janeiro in Brazil. It's really fun here! We're at the Carnaval. There's a big parade with music and dancing. We're wearing strange costumes, too! There's also a lot of amazing food. It's awesome! We're having a great time! Wish you were here!

Best wishes,
Stefan

Monkey Festival

ABOUT THE VIDEO

One town has a special festival for monkeys.

BEFORE YOU WATCH

Look at the photo. Circle two words you think you will hear to describe the monkeys.

angry   naughty   funny   colorful   big

WHILE YOU WATCH

A **Check your answers to the Before You Watch question.**

B **Watch the video again.** Circle **T** for True or **F** for False.

1. The festival is in Thailand. **T** **F**

2. Hanuman is the name of a place. **T** **F**

3. Some people at the festival wear costumes. **T** **F**

4. Tourists think that the monkeys are dangerous. **T** **F**

5. The tourist was angry when the monkey took his sunglasses. **T** **F**

AFTER YOU WATCH

Talk with a partner. Do you want to go to this festival? Do you know any other animal festivals?

Monkeys play at a temple during the Monkey Festival

Review Game 2

Play with 2–4 classmates. Take turns. Each classmate has a game counter. Toss a coin and move your counter.

Heads = move two squares
Tails = move one square

Can't answer? Miss a turn!

START!

1. What two things can your best friend do?

2. How many languages can you speak?

3. Who is this? What can he do?

4. Can you do a handstand?

5. What can you do at Dubai's Mall of the Emirates? Say three things.

6. What does haggling mean?

7. Which country uses pesos?

8. How much does a bag of potato chips cost in your country?

9. What are you doing now?

10. How many text messages do you send in one day?

11. Who is Robert Wood?

12. Who took this photo?

13. What's the weather like today?

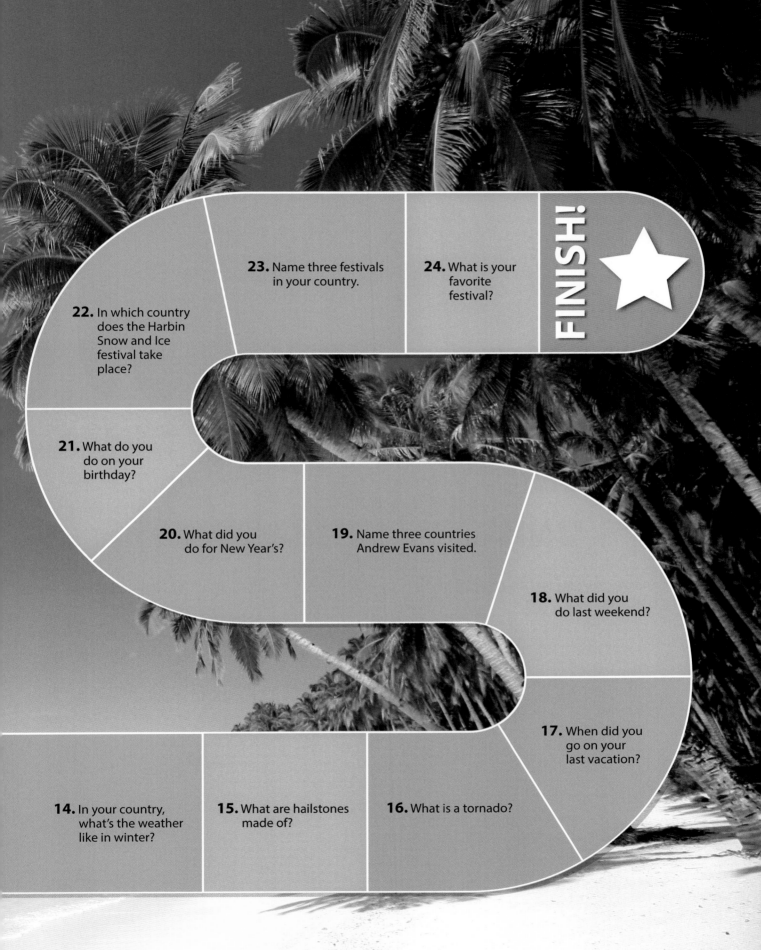

FINISH!

22. In which country does the Harbin Snow and Ice festival take place?

23. Name three festivals in your country.

24. What is your favorite festival?

21. What do you do on your birthday?

20. What did you do for New Year's?

19. Name three countries Andrew Evans visited.

18. What did you do last weekend?

17. When did you go on your last vacation?

14. In your country, what's the weather like in winter?

15. What are hailstones made of?

16. What is a tornado?

UNIT 3 WHERE'S THE SHARK?

Draw your partner's picture below. Compare the pictures.

UNIT 4 THIS IS MY FAMILY

Ask and answer questions to make your partner's family tree. Look at Lisa's family tree below to help you.

Lisa's Family Tree

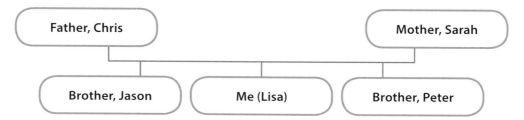

UNIT 5 I LIKE FRUIT!

Ask your partner what foods he or she likes and doesn't like. Remember the answers. Then play tic-tac-toe.

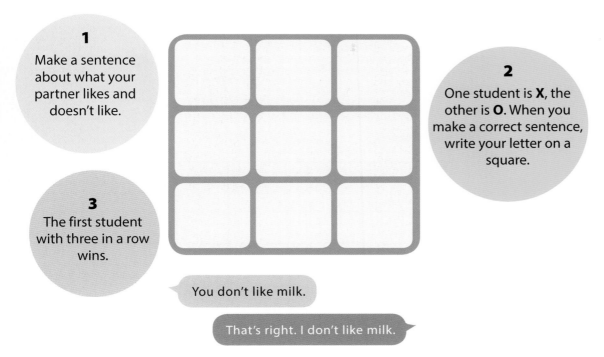

1
Make a sentence about what your partner likes and doesn't like.

2
One student is **X**, the other is **O**. When you make a correct sentence, write your letter on a square.

3
The first student with three in a row wins.

You don't like milk.

That's right. I don't like milk.

Create a menu using food that everyone in your group likes.

Meal	
Breakfast	
Lunch	
Dinner	

UNIT 9 WHAT ARE YOU DOING?

Complete the survey below and see your results.

Survey

IN ONE DAY HOW MANY...	0–2	3–6	7 OR MORE
...texts do you send?			
...games do you play on your phone?			
...hours do you spend on your laptop?			
...times do you check your email?			
...friends do you chat with online?			
...phone calls do you make?			

Survey Results

Count your points:

0–2 = 1 point

3–6 = 2 points

7 or more = 3 points

If your total is **1–7** you take your time with technology. You like to spend more time with people around you.

If your total is **8–14** you balance your time well between the online world and the real world.

If your total is **15 or more** you find it very hard to live without technology, even for a day!

Look at the picture below. Ask and answer questions about the pictures.

UNIT 10 WHAT'S THE WEATHER LIKE?

Ask and answer questions to complete the temperatures and weather conditions on the map below.

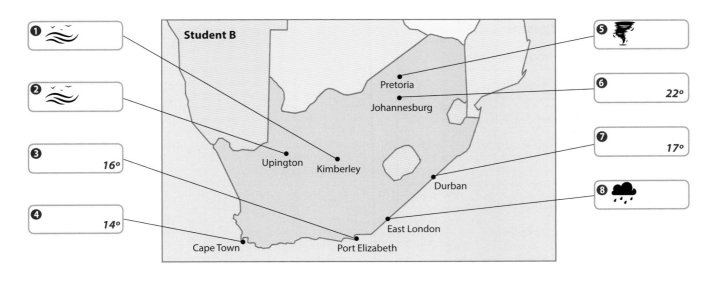

IRREGULAR PAST TENSE VERBS

BASE FORM	PAST FORM
become	became
bring	brought
buy	bought
catch	caught
choose	chose
come	came
cost	cost
cut	cut
draw	drew
drink	drank
drive	drove
eat	ate
fall	fell
feel	felt
fight	fought
find	found
fly	flew
get	got
give	gave
go	went
grow	grew
hear	heard
hurt	hurt
keep	kept
know	knew
let	let

BASE FORM	PAST FORM
lose	lost
make	made
mean	meant
meet	met
pay	paid
put	put
read	read
ride	rode
run	ran
say	said
see	saw
sell	sold
show	showed
sing	sang
sleep	slept
speak	spoke
swim	swam
take	took
teach	taught
tell	told
think	thought
throw	threw
understand	understood
wear	wore
win	won
write	wrote

LANGUAGE NOTES

UNIT 1 WHAT'S YOUR FAVORITE BAND?

WH- QUESTIONS (WHAT AND WHO)

What's	your my		favorite	TV show? movie?
Who's	his her			singer? actor?

POSSESSIVE DETERMINERS—THE VERB BE

My Your His Her	favorite sport **is** soccer.

POSSESSIVE 'S

Ana's favorite book **is** *Divergent*.

UNIT 2 MONKEYS ARE AMAZING!

THE VERB BE—PLURAL

Lizards Jaguars Frogs	**are**	noisy. amazing. beautiful.

NOUN PLURALS

Singular (=1)	Plural (>1)
lizard frog jaguar	lizards frogs jaguars

YES/NO QUESTIONS WITH BE—SHORT ANSWERS

Is	he she it	noisy?	Yes,	he she it	**is.**
			No,		**isn't.**
Are	they parrots	noisy?	Yes,	they	**are.**
			No,		**aren't.**

ASKING ABOUT ANIMALS

What's it like?	**It's** beautiful. **It's** shy.
How long does it live?	10 years.

UNIT 3 WHERE'S THE SHARK?

WH- QUESTIONS (*HOW MANY*)—*THERE IS/ARE*

How many sharks are there?	**There's** one (shark). **There are** two (sharks).

PREPOSITIONS OF LOCATION

It's	**under** the rock. **next to** the seaweed. **between** the seaweed **and** the rock.
They're	**in** the water. **in front of** the crab. **behind** the whale.

WH- QUESTIONS (*WHERE*)

Where's the octopus?
Where are the dolphins?

UNIT 4 THIS IS MY FAMILY.

DEMONSTRATIVES

This is **That's**	my	uncle. cousin.
These are **Those are**		brothers. parents.

YES/NO QUESTIONS WITH DEMONSTRATIVES—SHORT ANSWERS

Is	**this** **that**	your aunt?	Yes, **it is.** No, **it isn't.**
Are	**these** **those**	your cousins?	Yes, **they are.**

THE VERB *HAVE*

I **have** two sisters.
She **has** a brother.
They **have** a brother.

Do you **have** any brothers and sisters?	Yes, I **do**. No, I **don't**.
Does she **have** a brother?	Yes, she **does**. No, she **doesn't**.
Do they **have** any cousins?	Yes, they **do**. No, they **don't**.

do not = don't

does not = doesn't

UNIT 5 I LIKE FRUIT!

SIMPLE PRESENT (TO LIKE)

I **like** . . .	I **like** . . .
He/She/It **likes** . . .	He/She/It **likes** . . .
You/We/They **like** . . .	You / We / They **like** . . .

YES/NO QUESTIONS (TO LIKE) AND ANSWERS

Do	you they	**like** fruit?	Yes, I/we do. / No, I/we don't. Yes, they do. / No, they don't.
Does	he she	**like** rice?	Yes, he does. / No, he doesn't. Yes, she does. / No, she doesn't.

COUNTABLE AND UNCOUNTABLE NOUNS

countable	uncountable
chips	rice
sandwiches	coffee
apples	juice

OBJECT PRONOUNS (*IT, THEM*)

I **like** coffee.	I **like** it.
She **likes** sandwiches.	She **likes** them.

UNIT 6 WHAT TIME DO YOU GO TO SCHOOL?

SIMPLE PRESENT VERBS	
I get	I go
you get	you go
he gets	he goes
she gets	she goes
it gets	it goes
we get	we go
they get	they go

WH- QUESTIONS (WHAT TIME) AND ANSWERS

What time do	you they	get up?	I/we **usually** get up at 7:00. They **often** get up at 6:00.
What time does	he she		He **sometimes** gets up at 7:30. She **always** gets up at 7:15.

UNIT 7 CAN SQUIRRELS SKI?

CAN (ABILITY)

I You He She It We They	can can't	sing.

QUESTIONS WITH CAN (ABILITY)

Can	you he she it they	sing?	Yes,	I/we he she it they	can.
			No,		can't.

UNIT 8 HOW MUCH IS THIS T-SHIRT?

WH- QUESTIONS (*HOW MUCH*)

How much is	this that	T-shirt?	**It's** $12.
How much are	these those	jeans?	**They're** $29.

REFERENCE WORD—*ONE*

I want that CD.	→	I want that **one**.
I want the black sunglasses.	→	I want the black **ones**.

SIMPLE PRESENT (*WANT, WOULD LIKE*)

I You We They	**want** **don't want** **'d like**	that book.
He She	**wants** **doesn't want** **'d like**	those sunglasses.

POLITE *YES/NO* QUESTIONS (*WOULD LIKE*)—SHORT ANSWERS

Would	you he she they	**like** this baseball cap?	Yes,	I/we he she they	**would**.
			No,		**wouldn't**.

CAN (REQUESTS)

Can I see those T-shirts, please?	Sure. Here you go.

TOO (INTENSIFIER)

It's **too** big!

UNIT 9 WHAT ARE YOU DOING?

PRESENT PROGRESSIVE TENSE

I'm You're He's She's We're They're	**downloading** a video.

PRESENT PROGRESSIVE TENSE WITH *WH-* QUESTIONS

What are	you they	**doing**?	I'm/We're They're	**chatting** online.
What is	he she	**writing**?*	She's He's	**writing** an email.

PRESENT PROGRESSIVE TENSE WITH *YES/NO* QUESTIONS

Are	you they	**chatting** online?** **writing** an email?	Yes, I **am**. / No, I'm **not**. Yes, we **are**. / No, we're **not**. Yes, they **are**. / No, they're **not**.
Is	he she		Yes, she **is**. / No, she's **not**. Yes, he **is**. / No, he's **not**.

* Remember: if a verb ends in the letter *e*, drop the *e* before adding *-ing*.
  For example, *have—having, use—using*.

** The spelling in some words changes. For example, note the double consonant in
  chat—chatting.

UNIT 10 WHAT'S THE WEATHER LIKE?

WH- QUESTIONS (*WHAT + LIKE*)

What's the weather **like** in the summer?	It's cool and cloudy.

UNIT 11 I WENT TO AUSTRALIA!

SIMPLE PAST REGULAR VERBS

Most verbs add -ed	visit stay	visit**ed** stay**ed**
Verbs that have one syllable, a short vowel sound, and end with a single consonant	stop	stop**ped**
Verbs that end with a consonant + y	study	stud**ied**

SIMPLE PAST (*BE*)

I **was**
you **were**
he **was**
she **was**
it **was**
we **were**
they **were**

SIMPLE PAST IRREGULAR VERBS

do	**did**
eat	**ate**
get	**got**
go	**went**
have	**had**
ride	**rode**
see	**saw**
swim	**swam**
take	**took**
write	**wrote**

SIMPLE PAST INFORMATION QUESTIONS

How	**was**	your trip?
	were	the beaches?
What **did**	you he she they	do on vacation?
Where **did**		go?
Did		visit a temple?

SIMPLE PAST STATEMENTS

I He	**went** to Paris.
She They	**didn't go** to New York.

UNIT 12 WHAT DO YOU USUALLY DO FOR NEW YEAR'S?

SIMPLE PAST INFORMATION QUESTIONS

I went to a summer festival **during** the holidays.	
What did you do **on** New Year's Eve?	I **went** to a party.
Did you go on vacation **for** Diwali?	No, I didn't. I **stayed** at home.

Photo Credits

1 Jared Lim/500px, 3 EschCollection/Getty Images, 4–5 Abraham Nowitz/NGC, 6–7 Neleman/WIN-Initiative/Riser/Getty Images, 10 Alex Domanski/Reuters, 11 (tr) encikAn/Shutterstock, 11 (b) Gene Lower/Southcreek Global/ZUMAPRESS.com/Alamy, 12–13 Carlo Ramerino/Parallelozero/Aurora Photos, 15 Barry Tessman/NGC, 16–17 (bkg) Frans Lanting/NGC, 17 (bl) Roy Toft/NGC, 17 (br) M. & C. Photography/Getty Images, 18–19 Tim Laman/NGC, 20 (t) Frans Lanting/NGC, 20 (bl) Mark Bowler/Science Source, 20 (br) Richard Nowitz/NGC, 21 (tr) Pete Oxford/Danita Delimont Agent/Danita Delimont/Alamy, 21 (b) Tim Laman/NGC, 22–23 Frans Lanting/NGC, 23 (r) Adrian Sherratt/Alamy, 24 (cr) Encyclopaedia Britannica/Universal Images Group/Getty Images, 24 (br) Frans Lanting/NGC, 25 Christian Ziegler/Minden Pictures, 26–27 (bkg) Matias Klum/NGC, 27 (bc) Bill Curtsinger/NGC, 27 (br) Peter C Braddock/throughmyviewfinder/Getty Images, 29 (tr) George Grall/NGC, 30 (t) Cengage/NGC, 30 (bl) Joe Stancampiano/NGC, 30 (br) David Fleetham/Alamy, 32–33 Jeff Wildermuth/NGC, 33 (br) Constantinos Petrinos/Minden Pictures, 34 (br) Mauricio Handler/NGC, 35 Georgette Douwma/Photographer's Choice/Getty Images, 36–37 Touch Productions/National Geographic Channel, 39 Danielle Donders/Moment/Getty Images, 40 Vikram Raghuvanshi Photography/Vetta/Getty Images, 41 (tr) Michael N. Paras/age fotostock/Alamy, 42–43 Lisa Wiltse/Corbis, 45 Barcroft Media, 46–47 Fausto Giaccone/Anzenberger/Redux, 49 (c) Cengage Learning, 49 (br) Maximilian Stock Ltd/Getty Images, 50 Touch Productions: Human Footprint, 51 HiSunnySky/Shutterstock, 52–53 Carl Warner, 53 Carl Warner, 55 Andrew Kelly/Reuters Pictures, 56–57 Andersen Ross/IPNstock/Aurora Photos, 58–59 Thinkstock Images/Stockbyte/Getty Images, 60 LdF/Getty Images, 61 (tr) NASA, 61 (b) philia/Shutterstock, 62–63 Kate Cummings/NGC, 64 lculig/Shutterstock, 65 Philip Scott Andrews/NGC, 66–67 ?(bkg) Mattias Klum/NGC, (bl) Mauricio Handler/NGC, 68–69 AP Images/The Herald-Palladium/Don Campbell, 68 (br) Ricky Subiantoputra/Shutterstock, 71 NOVICA, 72 (t) Marco Grob/NGC, 72 (bl) Pillsbury Toaster Strudel/Handout/Getty Images, 72 (br) AP Images/Denis Farrell, 73 DigiPub/Moment Open/Getty Images, 73 (tr) philia/Shutterstock, 74–75 Laurentiu Garofeanu/Barcroft/Getty Images, 77 Henry Romero/Reuters, 78–79 Catherine Karnow/NGC, 81 Cengage Learning, 82 Martin Sasse/laif/Redux, 83 (tr) Tetra Images/Getty Images, 83 (b) Rostislav Glinsky/Shutterstock, 84–85 travelstock44/Getty Images, 86 Pedro Rufo/Shutterstock, 87 Douglas Pearson/Getty Images, 88–89 Jonathan Alcorn/Reuters, 91 Image Source/Getty Images, 92 (bkg) Rebecca Drobis/NGC, 92 (br) Cengage/NGC, 93 (tr) Photos 12/Alamy, 94–95 Brian Snyde/Reuters, 96 (cl) MakerBot®, 96 (b) Radu Bercan/Shutterstock, 97 (c) Chris McLennan Photography, 97 (b) Chris McLennan Photography, 98–99 Julie Mayfeng/NGC, 99 (tr) meaculpa_1/Shutterstock, 102 (t) Eric Meola/The Image Bank/Getty Images, 102 (bl) Eric Nguyen/Science Source, 102 (br) kazoka/Shutterstock, 103 Mark Duffy/NGC, 104–105 Roger Hill/Barcroft USA/Getty Images, 106 (tr) fotokon/Getty Images, 106 (br) photogerson/Shutterstock, 107 Gene Blevins/Reuters Pictures, 108–109 Sean Davey/Aurora Photos, 110–111 Mark A.Johnson/Ivy/Corbis, 112 Brian Gratwicke, 113 (tr) Syda Productions/Shutterstock, 113 (b) Ikpro/Shutterstock, 114–115 Jo-Anne McArthur/Redux, 116 wolfmaster13/Shutterstock, 117 (bkg) Andrew Evans/NGC, 117 (c) BigBigbb1/Shutterstock, 118–119 Nutexzles/Moment Select/Getty Images, 120–121 John Stanmeyer LLC/NGC, 121 (tr) R.M. Nunes/Shutterstock, 122 (t) Tino Soriano/NGC, 122 (bl) Melissa Farlow/NGC, 122 (br) Nacho Doce/Reuters, 123 Frederic Nebinger/Getty Images, 124–125 Cancan Chu/Getty Images News/Getty Images, 126 (br) Migel/Shutterstock, 127 Sukree Sukplang/Reuters, 128–129 (bkg) photogerson/Shuterstock, (tl) Laurentiu Garofeanu/Barcroft/Getty Images, (bl) Chris McLennan Photography

NGC = National Geographic Creative

Art Credits

8, 18, 28, 38, 48, 58, 70, 80, 90, 93, 100, 110, 120, 133 Raketshop, 29, 31, 66-67, 128–129, 130 Lachina, **Graphic Symbols: Unit 1** Ints Vikmanis/Shutterstock, WonderfulPixel/Shutterstock, Denis Maliugin/Shutterstock, grmarc/Shutterstock, Bioraven/Shutterstock, Kapreski/Shutterstock, **Unit 2** Voropaev Vasiliy/Shutterstock, hippo/Shutterstock, **Unit 5** bioraven/Shutterstock, Bakai/Shutterstock, **Unit 6** Jovanovic Dejan/Shutterstock, gst/Shutterstock, Nikiteev_Konstantin/Shutterstock, **Unit 7** Aliaksandr Radzko/Shutterstock, snorks/Shutterstock, Nikiteev_Konstantin/Shutterstock, Happy Art/Shutterstock, **Unit 8** Hein Nouwens/Shutterstock, pnDl/Shutterstock, WonderfulPixel/Shutterstock, **Unit 9** Epsicons/Shutterstock, iconspro/Shutterstock, Epsicons/Shutterstock, **Unit 10** Kapreski/Shutterstock, **Unit 12** MuchMania/Shutterstock, Kapreski/Shutterstock

Acknowledgments

The authors and publisher would like to thank the following individuals and organizations who offered many helpful insights, ideas, and suggestions during the development of **Time Zones**.

Asia and Europe

Phil Woodall, Aoyama Gakuin Senior High School; **Suzette Buxmann**, Aston A+; **Wayne Fong**, Aston English; Berlitz China; Berlitz Germany; Berlitz Hong Kong; Berlitz Japan; Berlitz Singapore; **Anothai Jetsadu**, Cha-am Khunying Nuangburi School; **Rui-Hua Hsu**, Chi Yong High School; **Gary Darnell**, DEU Private School, Izmir; **Hwang Soon Hee, Irean Yeon, Junhee Im, Seungeun Jung**, Eun Seok Elementary School; **Hyun Ah Park**, Gachon University; **Hsi-Tzu Hung**, Hwa Hsia Institute of Technology; **Kate Sato**, Kitopia English School; **Daniel Stewart**, Kaisei Junior and Senior High School; **Haruko Morimoto, Ken Ip**, Mejiro Kenshin Junior and Senior High School; **Sovoan Sem**, Milky Way School; **Shu-Yi Chang**, Ming Dao High School; **Ludwig Tan**, National Institute of Education; **Tao Rui, Yuan Wei Hua**, New Oriental Education & Technology Group; **Tom Fast**, Okayama Gakugeikan High School; **Yu-Ping Luo**, Oriental Institute of Technology; **Jutamas**, Prakhanong Pittayalai School; **Akira Yasuhara**, Rikkyo Ikebukuro Junior and Senior High School; **Matthew Rhoda**, Sakuragaoka Junior and Senior High School; **Michael Raship, Nicholas Canales**, Scientific Education Group Co; **Andrew O'Brien**, Second Kyoritsu Girls Junior and Senior High School; **Atsuko Okada**, Shinagawa Joshi Gakuin Junior and Senior High School; **Sheila Yu**, Shin Min High School; **Stewart Dorward**, Shumei Junior and Senior High School; **Gaenor Hardy**, Star English Centres; **Philip Chandler, Thomas Campagna**, Tama University Meguro Junior and Senior High School; **Lois Wang**, Teachall English; **Iwao Arai, James Daly, Satomi Kishi**, Tokyo City University Junior and Senior High School; **Jason May**, Tokyo Seitoku University High School; **Amnoui Jaimipak**, Triamudomsuksapattanakarn Chiangrai School; **Jonee de Leon**, Universal English Center; **Thiwaphorn Tharawatcharasart**, Uthaiwitthayakhom School; **Richard Ascough**, Wayo Women's University; **Kirvin Andrew Dyer**, Yan Ping High School

The Americas

Allynne Fraemam, Flávia Carneiro, Jonathan Reinaux, Mônica Carvalho, ABA; **Antonio Fernando Pinho**, Academia De Idiomas; **Wilmer Escobar**, Academia Militar; **Adriana Rupp, Denise Silva, Jorge Mendes**, ACBEU; **Rebecca Gonzalez**, AIF Systems English Language Institute; **Camila Vidal Suárez, Adriana Yaffe, Andrea da Silva, Bruno Oliveri, Diego A. Fábregas Acosta, Fabiana Hernandez, Florencia Barrios, Ignacio Silveira Trabal, Lucía Greco Castro, Lucy Pintos, Silvia Laborde**, Alianza Cultural Uruguay Estados Unidos; **Adriana Alvarez**, ASICANA; **Corina C. Machado Correa, Silvia Helena R. D. Corrêa, Mariana M. Paglione Vedana**, Associacao Alumni; Berlitz, Colombia; Berlitz Mexico; Berlitz Peru; Berlitz US; **Simone Ashton**, Britanic Madalena; **Keith Astle**, Britanic Piedade; **Dulce Capiberibe**, Britanic Setúbal; **Matthew Gerard O'Conner**, Britanic Setúbal; **Viviane Remígio**, Britanic Setúbal; **Adriana da Silva, Ana Raquel F. F. Campos, Ebenezer Macario, Giselle Schimaichel, Larissa Platinetti, Miriam Alves Carnieletto, Selma Oliveira**, Centro Cultural Brasil Estados Unidos CCBEU; **Amiris Helena**, CCDA; **Alexandra Nancy Lake Sawada, Ana Tereza R. P. Moreira, Denise Helena Monteiro, Larissa Ferreria, Patricia Mckay Aronis**, CELLEP; **Claudia Patricia Gutierrez, Edna Zapata, Leslie Cortés, Silvia Elena Martinez, Yesid Londoño**, Centro Colombo Americano-Medellin; **Gabriel Villamar Then**, Centro Educativo los Prados; **Monica Lugo**, Centro Escolar Versalles; **Adriane Caldas, Simone Raupp, Sylvia Formoso**, Colégio Anchieta; **José Olavo de Amorim**, Colégio Bandeirantes; **Dionisio Alfredo Meza Solar**, Colegio Cultural I; **Madson Gois Diniz**, Colegio De Aplicação; **Ilonka Diaz, Melenie Gonzalez**, Colegio Dominico Espanol; **Laura Monica Cadena, Rebeca Perez**, Colegio Franco Ingles; **Jedinson Trujillo**, Colegio Guías; **Christophe Flaz, Isauro Sanchez Gutierrez**, Colegio Iglesa Bautista Fundamenta; **Ayrton Lambert**, Colégio II Peretz; **Samuel Jean Baptiste**, Colegio Instituto Montessori; **Beatriz Galvez, Evelyn Melendez**, Colegio Los Olivos; **Carlos Gomez, Diana Herrera Ramirez, Diana Pedraza Aguirre, Karol Bibana Hutado Morales**, Colegio Santa Luisa; **Marta Segui Rivas**, Colegio Velmont; **Thays Ladosky**, DAMAS; **Amalia Vasquez, Ana Palencia, Fernando de Leon, Isabel Cubilla, Leonel Zapata, Lorena Chavarria, Maria Adames**, English Access Microscholarship Program; **Rosângela Duarte Dos Santos**, English Space; **Walter Junior Ribeiro Silva**, Friends Language Center; **Luis Reynaldo Frias**, Harvard Institute; **Carlos Olavo Queiroz Guimarães, Elisa Borges, Patricia Martins, Lilian Bluvol Vaisman, Samara Camilo Tomé Costa**, IBEU; **Gustavo Sardo, João Carlos Queiroz Furtado, Rafael Bastos, Vanessa Rangel**, IBLE; **Graciela Martin**, ICANA (BELGRANO); **Carlos Santanna, Elizabeth Gonçalves**, ICBEU; **Inês Greve Milke, João Alfredo Bergmann**, Instituto Cultural Brasileiro Norte-Americano; **Tarsis Perez**, ICDA-Instituto Cultural Dominico Americano; **Cynthia Marquez, Guillermo Cortez, Ivan Quinteros, Luis Morales R, Melissa Lopez, Patricia Perez, Rebeca de Arrue, Rebeca Martinez de Arrue**, Instituto Guatemalteco Americano; **Renata Lucia Cardoso**, Instituto Natural de Desenvolvimento Infantil; **Graciela Nobile**, Instituto San Diego; **Walter Guevara**, Pio XII; **Juan Omar Valdez**, Professional Training Systems; **Carlos Carmona, Eugenio Altieri, Regan Albertson**, Progressive English Services; **Raul Billini**, Prolingua; **Juan Manuel Marin, Luisa Fecuanda Infort, Maria Consuelo Arauijo**, Providencia; **Carmen Gehrke**, Quatrum, Porto Alegre; **Rodrigo Rezende**, Seven; **Lcuciano Joel del Rosario**, St. José School; **Sabino Morla**, UASD; **Silvia Regina D'Andrea**, União Cultural Brasil-Estados Unidos; **Ruth Salomon- Barkemeyer**, Unilínguas Sao Leopoldo; **Anatalia Souza, Livia Rebelo**, UNIME-Ingles Para Criancas- Salvador; **Andrei dos Santos Cunha, Brigitte Mund, Gislaine Deckmann, Jeane Blume Cortezia, Rosana Gusmão**, Unisinos; **Diego Pérez**, Universidad de Ibague; **Beatriz Daldosso Felippe**, U.S. Idiomas Universe School

Ian Purdon would like to thank you the reader for choosing Time Zones to learn English. I truly hope you enjoy our course, make swift progress at school, achieve your goals, and find out new and exciting facts about the world along the way.

I would also like to thank the editors at National Geographic Learning for all their hard work and dedication to making this second edition a success.

Best wishes to you all!